John Jones

# An impartial Narrative of each Engagement which took Place between His Majesty's Forces

### And the Rebels, during the Irish Rebellion, 1798 - Part 1, Edition 4

John Jones

**An impartial Narrative of each Engagement which took Place between His Majesty's Forces
And the Rebels, during the Irish Rebellion, 1798 - Part 1, Edition 4**

ISBN/EAN: 9783337216559

Printed in Europe, USA, Canada, Australia, Japan

Cover: Foto ©ninafisch / pixelio.de

More available books at **www.hansebooks.com**

AN IMPARTIAL
# NARRATIVE
OF EACH
# ENGAGEMENT
WHICH TOOK PLACE BETWEEN
## HIS MAJESTY'S FORCES
AND THE
# REBELS,
DURING
# The Irish Rebellion,
## 1798.
INCLUDING VERY INTERESTING INFORMATION
NOT BEFORE MADE PUBLIC.

---

*CAREFULLY COLLECTED*
## FROM AUTHENTIC LETTERS,
BY JOHN JONES.

---

Embellished with Engravings of the Battles of Arklow and Tara-Hill.

THE FOURTH EDITION.

---

PART I.

---

DUBLIN:
Printed and Sold by John Jones,
91, BRIDE-STREET.

1800.

# PREFACE.

The Editor with the moſt profound reſpect, ſubmits to the Public the following NARRATIVE.—It forms a ſmall portion of a more extended work, calculated to contain the particulars of every remarkable occurrence, connected with the Rebellion, which happened in the Year Ninety Eight;—a year which will conſtitute an EPOCH in the hiſtory of Ireland, and the events of which ought to be univerſally known.

The moment of action is not the moſt favourable to accuracy of detail:—Notwithſtanding the pureſt intentions and the moſt ſcrupulous regard to truth, much will remain for candour to extenuate and information to ſupply. Impreſſed with this ſentiment, and feeling the importance of the ſubject, the Editor has waited till

till the feafon of tranquility, and now prefents to the public eye, the produce of his exertions. He wifhed to poftpone the Publication in order to complete it, but he yields to the entreaties of his Friends, and finds it neceffary to make fome facrifice to the eagernefs of public curiofity: The remaining part is in preparation for the Prefs, and as he continues to be fupplied by thofe who were witneffes at the tranfactions, and confequently moft capable of communicating correct intelligence, he hopes foon to accomplifh his defign.

The Reader will perceive from the following fpecimen, that the accounts of the Battles are not arranged in chronological order; neither do they boaft of any great pretenfions to literary merit; but they will be found to have a recommendation

more

more valuable than either—AUTHEN-TICITY. The Editor was less solicitous about the style of the work, than the truth of it, and where, upon investigation, the matter conveyed to him proved correct, he has given it in the language of his correspondent.

If History be, as it has been elegantly described, " Philosophy teaching by Example,"—what example more necessary to be held out to public view, and transmitted to posterity, than that which shews the dreadful effects of a Revolution attempted by force, where the visionary politician enjoys for so short a time his sanguinary triumph—suspected even by those whom he calls his friends, he is superseded by such as are more ferocious than himself, while the fury of Fanaticism equally destroys *his* prospects in the mad effort to exterminate

terminate one religion and substitute another.

The perusal of such transactions must suggest useful reflections. The surviving Loyalist will rejoice in the triumph of *law* and the restoration of *order*. The surviving Rebel will repent of his folly, and enjoy the comforts which Law and Order distribute.

Such are the motives, and such the object which influence the Editor of this little Work. From those who may approve of it, and whose situation and leisure furnish the opportunity, he requests further assistance. Particulars of Engagements, not included in this part, will be thankfully received, and due attention paid to them in the subsequent Publications.

CONTENTS.

## OF PART I.

|  | Page. |
|---|---|
| Description of Clonard, | 3 |
| Battle of Timahoe, | 9 |
| Junction of the Wexford and Kildare Rebels, | 12 |
| Battle of Clonard, | ib. |
| Mrs. Tyrrell's sufferings while prisoner with the rebels, | 23 |
| Character of Col. Perry and Priest Kearns who were executed, | 30 |

### LETTERS.

| I. Battle of Carlow, | 34 |
|---|---|
| II. Battle of Ross, | 38 |
| III. Battle of Castlecomber, &c. | 41 |
| IV. Battle of Kilcomney, | 48 |
| V. Second Account of the Battle of Kilcomney, | 52 |
| VI. Battle of Saintfield, | 57 |
| VII. Battle of Kilbeggan, | 60 |

### OFFICIAL ACCOUNTS.

| Battle of Naas, | 63 |
|---|---|
| Battle of Kilcullen, | 65 |
| Battle of Hacket's-town, | 67 |

### LETTERS.

| VIII. Battle of Arklow, | 70 |
|---|---|

*Account*

IX. *Account of the depredations of the Rebels at Gorey—their sacrilegious treatment of the Church, in which they immolated two Protestants,* - 73

X. *Situation of the Rebels on Vinegar-Hill,* 75
*Description of Vinegar-Hill——the Battle,* 76

XI. *Accurate detail of the effects of the Rebellion in the County of Wexford,* - 78
*Battle of Oulart,* - - - 80
*Attack at Enniscorthy,* - - ib.
*Battle of the Three Rocks,* - - 81
*Atrocities of the Rebels and the sufferings of the Loyalists in Wexford, &c.* - 83
*Names of Clergymen and principal Gentlemen put to death,* - - 86

## APPENDIX.

*Copy of an Affidavit made before the Right Hon. the Lord Mayor of the City of Dublin, relative to the attack on Prosperous,* 87
*Account of the murder of Capt. Swayne— Burning of the Barracks, and the cries of the Soldiers consumed therein— Murder of Messrs. Stamer and Brewer, &c.*

# A NARRATIVE

OF THE MOST IMPORTANT

# ENGAGEMENTS

DURING

# The Irish Rebellion,

1798.

PART I.

---

CLONARD is situate about Twenty-five miles from Dublin, on the Western road leading to Mullingar. Tho' constituted a post town, it is a very small village, consisting of an Inn and a few thatched houses; but from its situation, being on the confines of two counties, Kildare and Meath, and having a bridge across the river Boyne, which opens a communication from Dublin

Dublin to Westmeath, and from thence to Athlone and the Province of Connaught, it must be considered as a very important pass in all times of commotion and war. On the Dublin side of the town is situated the mansion house of the Tyrrell family, and at present belongs to *John Tyrrell*, Esq. It is an old fashioned house, fronting the road, from which it is separated by a high wall and a court yard; having an extensive garden upon its right, and a sheet of water upon the left.—Mr. John Tyrrell, being a Magistrate of both counties, Kildare and Meath, and having exerted himself early to suppress the disturbances which were occasioned by the Defenders, naturally became an object of their resentment, and having been repeatedly menaced with an attack, he fortified his house by building up the original hall door, opening another, which might flank the approach to the house, and barricading all the lower windows, so as to render them musquet proof.

Upon the institution of the yeomenry, Mr. John Tyrrell was honoured with a commission

to

to raise a corps of cavalry, which was immediately embodied, under the title of the *Clonard cavalry*, and Thomas Tyrrell, and Thomas Barlow, Esqs. were appointed Lieutenants. This corps soon distinguished itself by its unwearied exertions to preserve the peace of the neighbourhood; but in the course of the Spring of 1798, Mr. John Tyrrell the Captain, receiving positive information of a conspiracy to take away his life, thought it prudent to retire with his family into England.

The command of the corps consequently devolved upon Mr. Thomas Tyrrell, the first Lieutenant, who had also at this critical period been appointed High Sheriff of the county of Kildare—Upon the tenth of May 1798, he received an official letter, ordering the Clonard cavalry upon permanent duty: in this emergency Mr. Thomas Tyrrell, finding his own house at Kilreiny, about one mile and a half from Clonard inconvenient, and in truth indefensible from its situation, removed with his family to his kinsman's house at Clonard, before described,

where

where he mounted a guard of one Serjeant and 18 men who were to be relieved every week.

Orders were about the same time issued to Captain O' Ferral, of the Ballina cavalry, to mount a permanent guard at Johnstown, near the Nineteen-mile house, which were accordingly complied with: but upon the 16th of May, reports of a general rising having been circulated, and being corroborated by encreasing outrages in the neighbourhood, Captain O' Ferral was permitted to fall back from Johnstown to Clonard in the night time for protection; repairing to Johnstown at four o'clock in the morning, and retiring to Clonard in the evening.

In this way matters went on for some time, when the country becoming still more disturbed and apprehensions of an attack upon Clonard becoming more serious, Lieutenant Thomas Tyrrell repaired to Dublin with an escort of his corps, leaving the command at Clonard with Lieutenant Barlow. The object of this visit to Dublin, was to represent to Government the situation of that part of the country, the daily apprehensions henfions of an attack, and the neceffity of a reinforcement. Lord Caftlereagh, to whom thefe reprefentations were made, anfwered, that under the exifting circumftances no force could be fent to Clonard, but Mr. Thomas Tyrrell was authorized to raife fome Supplementaries, for whom he would be fupplied with arms and ammunition.

Pending this application in Dublin, viz. upon the 29th of May the rebels affembled to the number of 800 in the village of Carbery, five miles from Clonard, where they burned the Proteftant Charter School and feveral houfes; they then proceeded through Johnftown, burning and deftroying the houfe of every Proteftant near the road. Towards evening they halted at a place called Gurteen, where they deftroyed the houfe of Mr. Francis Metcalf.—When intelligence of thefe tranfactions reached Clonard, Lieutenant Barlow marched out with a party of the guard, and being joined by Captain O' Ferrall they went in purfuit of the rebels, but did not overtake them, until they had halted at Gurteen, where

where they had taken a very advantageous position upon each side of a narrow road, behind strong quickset hedges, so that cavalry could not approach them with any prospect of success. Lieutenant Barlow halted his men, and then advancing some paces towards the enemy, took off his helmet, and challenged them to come forward. They however declined leaving their entrenchments, and night approaching, the yeomenry with great reluctance returned to their guard house.

On the 30th of May, Lieutenant Thomas Tyrrell arrived safe from Dublin, with his escort, carabines for the troop, musquets for the supplementaries and a quantity of ammunition. The next day he enrolled nineteen well affected Protestants to act as supplementaries and dismounted.

By this time the rebels had collected a very considerable force, and every night committed some outrage and depredation. They encamped upon an Island in the bog of Timahoe, and also at Mucklin and Dreihid; they plundered almost every

every house in the neighbourhood of their respective places, drove away all the fat cattle and horses they could meet, and intercepted the supplies for the Dublin market.

## BATTLE OF TIMAHOE.

Government being apprized of these proceedings, dispatched General Champagne to Clonard, where he arrived upon the 6th of June; and after consulting with Lieutenant Tyrrell, was escorted by him to Edenderry, where the Gen. expected a detachment of the Limerick militia; but being disappointed in this respect, an express was sent to Philipstown to hasten the reinforcement, which arrived at Edenderry upon the evening of the 7th; and on the next day, General Champagne, having arranged his plan of operations, marched from Edenderry, with the following forces: A detachment of the Limerick militia, under Lieutenant Colonel Gough; the Cooleſtown yeomen cavalry, under Captain Wakely and Lieutenant Cartland; the Canal legion, under Lieutenant Adam Williams; the Clonard cavalry, Lieutenant T. Tyrrell; and the

the Ballina cavalry, Captain O'Ferrall. Thefe feveral corps were diftributed, fo as that the cavalry fhould furround the bog of Timahoe, while the infantry attacked the camp upon the Ifland: This judicious plan was completely executed—the conteft was obftinate for fome time, owing to the fmall number of the infantry, who led on the attack; but their firmnefs and difcipline fupplying the want of numbers, the Limerick, headed by the gallant Colonel Gough, and ably fupported by Lieutenant Williams, marched into the entrenchments, drove the rebels from their camp, who were attacked in their flight by the cavalry and many of them put to death. The camp was entirely deftroyed, and a great quantity of prifoners and confiderable booty were carried off by the victors!

On the 29th of June, Lieutenant Tyrrell having received information that a large body of rebels had ftationed themfelves upon a hill near his dwelling-houfe at Kilreiny, and had committed various robberies in the courfe of the preceding night,

night, he went to Kinnegad to solicit a reinforcement, and sent an express to Edenderry for a force to co-operate with him. The Kinnegad yeomen cavalry, under Lieutenant Houghton, and a small party of the Northumberland Fencibles immediately marched with Lieutenant Tyrrell to Clonard, and from thence being joined by his own corps, he proceeded to *Fox's hill*, where the rebels were posted to the amount of 600—The attack was begun by the Clonard Supplementaries, who displayed great steadiness upon this occasion: the Kinnegad corps and the Northumberlands supported the attack with great zeal, and the Edenderry force, consisting of a detachment of the Limerick, Lieutenant Colonel Gough, the Cooleftown cavalry, Captain Wakely, and the Canal legion, Lieutenant Williams, having fallen upon the rebels from the opposite side, they were routed with considerable slaughter. Their commander, one *Casey*, his brother and another Leader were killed in this action, and their bodies brought to Edenderry, where they were exposed for several days.

*JUNCTION*

## JUNCTION OF THE WEXFORD AND KILDARE REBELS.

It might have been hoped that these successas would have established tranquility in this neighbourhood, and probably such effects would have followed the military exertions, were it not for the irruption of a large column of Wexford rebels into Kildare, under the command of Colonel *Perry*, who being immediately joined by Colonel *Aylmer*,‡ commanding the rebel camp at Prosperous, was prevailed upon to abandon his intention of penetrating into the North, and to adapt a plan suggested by *Aylmer*, of attacking Clonard, pushing on from thence by Kilbeggan to the Shannon and surprising Athlone. In pursuance of this plan, the rebel forces amounting to 4000 men made a movement towards Clonard.

## BATTLE OF CLONARD.

Lieutenant Tyrrell was totally unapprized of the intention, or motions of the enemy:— his guard were extremely vigilant during each night, but not apprehending any danger in the

‡ *Perry and Aylmer were thus appointed by the rebels.*

day time, they frequently difperfed through the village for the purpofe of recreation and refrefhment. This happened to be the cafe with many of his men upon Wednefday morning the 11th of July, on which day about eleven o'clock, Mr. *Richard Allen* galloped into the Court, and brought intelligence that he was purfued by a picquet guard of the rebels, whom he narrowly efcaped, as they were well mounted; and he was confident a confiderable force was approaching. The alarm was inftantly given—every exertion was made to collect the fcattered men, and parties were ftationed in the moft advantageous pofitions. As the enemy were expected from the Dublin fide, fix of the corps (including Mr. Allen and Thomas Tyrrell, junr. the Lieutenant', fon, and only fifteen years of age) took poffeffion of an old Turret at the extremity of the garden, and which commanded the road. Such was the rapidity with which the rebels advanced, that the firing actually commenced from this quarter upon their cavalry before the entire guard could be collected, and the gate leading into the court yard

yard was under such necessity closed to the exclusion of several, so that when Lieutenant Tyrrell came to ascertain his strength, he found he had only *Twenty-seven* men, including his own three sons, the eldest of whom was only seventeen years old! Such a critical situation required the coolness of a man inured to military danger, and all the exertion, firmness and skill of a veteran soldier. But although Lieutenant Tyrrell never had served in the army, his own good sense supplied the want of experience, and his native courage furnished resources adequate to the magnitude of the occasion. He found his men as zealous as himself, determined to maintain their post and discharge their duty to their King and Country, or fall in such a glorious cause. After sending a supply of ammunition to the advanced post at the Turret, and stationing other out-posts, he retired into the house with the main body, from which he selected the best marksmen; and placing them at particular windows gave directions that they should not fire without having their object covered, he had the rest of

the

the men secured behind the walls and inceffantly employed in loading mufkets and carabines for the markfmen at the windows.

The firing as we have obferved commenced from the Turret at the extremity of the garden. About 300 of the rebel cavalry, lead on by one *Farrell* formed their advanced guard, and approached the Turret in a fmart trot, without appearing to apprehend any danger. The firft fhot was fired by young Mr. Tyrrell, which mortally wounded Farrell, and being followed by a general difcharge from the reft among the body of the cavalry, threw them into great confufion, in which ftate they fled out of the reach of the firing. The infantry however coming up, many of them contrived to pafs the Turret under cover of the wall, and numbers were pofted behind a thick hedge on the oppofite fide of the road, from which they kept up a fmart fire againft the Turret, but without doing any material mifchief.

The infantry who had paffed the Turret being joined by a party who came by a crofs road (for it feems their plan was to furround the houfe by advancing in different directions) they stationed a guard upon the bridge to prevent any reinforcement arriving in that direction. About ten or a dozen of this guard were in a very few minutes shot by the markſmen from the windows, upon which the reſt fled; not one of the rebels ventured afterwards to appear upon the bridge, ſo that the communication with the Weſtern road was in a great meaſure preſerved, the importance of which to the little garriſon in Clonard will appear in the event of the day.

The enemy being thus defeated in their firſt onſet in both points of attack, became exaſperated to an extravagant pitch of fury—and determined upon the moſt ſavage revenge. A large party contrived to penetrate into the garden, by the rere, and ſome of them immediately ruſhed into the Turret. The yeomen ſtationed there were upon an upper floor—they had the precaution to drag up the ladder by which they aſcended;—the rebels endeavoured to climb upon each other, ſo as to reach the upper ſtory, but they were killed as faſt as they appeared;

others

others then ran their pikes through the cieling, and fired shots but without effect—the conflict was obstinate—twenty seven of the rebels lay dead on the ground floor, when at length, a quantity of straw was brought and set on fire. The building was soon in flames; two of the yeomen. Mr. Michael Cusack, and Mr. George Tyrrell, endeavouring to force their way through the smoke were immediately put to death; the rest of the party, viz. Mr. Allen, young Mr. T. Tyrrell, and two others escaped, by leaping from a window twenty foot high into an hay-yard, from whence under cover of a wall which divided it from the garden they escaped into the house.

Having succeeded so well by the effect of conflagration, the enemy set fire to the toll-house and some other cabins on the left near the bridge, for the purpose of embarrasing and confusing the garrison; during this operation, they were seen throwing their dead into the flames, for the purpose, it was thought of evading discovery.

The battle had now lasted near six hours: about five in the evening, the approach of succour was descried from the house—the hopes of all were elevated, and they fought with renovated vigour.

One of the guard who had been excluded by the sudden shutting of the gates in the morning, finding he could be of no other use, repaired to Kinnegad, represented the situation of his friends at Clonard, upon which fourteen of the Kinnegad infantry, under Lieutenant Houghton, and eleven Northumberland Fencibles, under the command of a Serjeant, immediately collected, and with great gallantry marched for Clonard. The communication by the bridge having been kept open in the manner before related, Lieutenant Tyrrell sallied from the house, and soon effected a junction with this reinforcement. A few vollies completely cleared the roads, and having then placed the Northumberland and Kinnegad men in such situations as most effectually to gall the enemy in their retreat from the garden, the

Lieutenant

Lieutenant undertook in perſon, the hazardous enterpriſe of diſlodging them from thence.

At this time it is ſuppoſed there were 400 rebels in the garden; numbers of them were poſted upon a mount planted with old fir trees, which afforded confiderable protection, and many lay concealed behind a privet hedge, from whence they could diſtinctly ſee every perſon who entered the garden, tho' they could not be ſeen themſelves—Lieutenant Tyrrell at the head of a few picked men, ruſhed into the garden; and was received by a general diſcharge from both parties of the enemy: no time was loſt in attacking the party behind the hedge, who being defeated, retired to the mount;—here the action again became warm, the rebels appeared determined to maintain the advantage of their ſituation, and the yeomen, tho' fatigued with the labour of the day, could not think of retiring. Six of them were badly wounded, among whom was Mr. Richard Allen who had ſo gallantly defended the Turret—a ball paſſed thro' his left arm, and entered his ſide; his comrades ſtill perſevered with

with the most undaunted courage, and supporting a steady and well directed fire against the mount, the enemy were at length dispersed, and in their flight were met by the Northumberland and Kinnegad corps who made great havoc among them.

The victory was now complete—as glorious an atchievement, we will venture to say, as occurred during the whole rebellion, and for which the gallant officers and men can never be too much applauded, whether we consider it as an unexampled display of genuine loyalty and true courage, or estimate its value from its immense importance to that part of the country, and the kingdom at large. It was the first check which the United army of Wexford and Kildare experienced, and proved the fore-runner of those multiplied defeats which terminated in its total dispersion.

### MRS. TYRRELLS's SUFFERINGS WHILE PRISONER WITH THE REBELS.

After the battle it might have been expected that the little garrison would have given themselves

selves up to an excess of joy; but the breast of their commander was filled with anxious solicitude—the partner of his heart—his wife; the mother of those three gallant youths, who mixed in the hottest scenes of the day, was absent the whole time, and no tidings of her had reached the garrison. The men sympathised with the husband and the children, and success was thought incomplete, until she was restored to their embraces.

Probably the reader may participate somewhat of a similar feeling, and desire some gratification from a brief narrative of the circumstances attending the lady while in possession of the rebels.

On the morning of the 11th of July, about the hour that the guard dispersed, as we have before mentioned, Mrs. Tyrrell went in her carriage from Clonard to her own house at Kilreiny upon some domestic concerns—she soon heard the rebels were coming, and speedily drove back with the hope of reaching Clonard before them.

them. In this however she was disappointed; the noise of musquetry convinced her of the impractability of this attempt. The servant was ordered to turn about and drive to Kilreiny, from whence she intended to send an express to Edenderry—she had not however proceeded many yards, when the carriage was overtaken by two men on horseback, armed with drawn swords, who with oaths and menaces ordered the servant to stop—They turned the carriage back towards Clonard until they overtook about 200 men armed with pikes, a few musquets and some swords. They searched the carriage for arms but did not find any. Mrs. Tyrrell describes the men as a ragged, wretched looking banditti: three of them armed with musquets mounted the boot of the carriage; three more got behind it—and in this manner attended by a great crowd, the carriage was drove two miles round to the high road leading from Dublin to Clonard: here they kept her a prisoner, notwithstanding her frequent entreaties to be enlarged; she at one time apprehended the pike-men would cut her to pieces, as

they

they quarrelled among themselves, some being disposed to treat her with civility—others the reverse—after some time she prevailed upon them to permit her to retire into a cabin, the inhabitants of which knew her, and two men armed with musquets were placed as centries. She there remained, until the rebels were defeated at Clonard, when the whole body upon their retreat assembled at the cabin; one of the rebel officers came in, and desired Mrs. Tyrrell to get into her carriage; she asked for what purpose? He replied, that she must go with them; she entreated him to permit her to remain where she was, and that her carriage and horses were at his service; he for some time denied her request: but falling on her knees to supplicate him, he told her she might stay. He then withdrew, but immediately a great common fellow came in, seized her by the arm, dragged her to the door, and desired some men to lift her upon a horse which had been provided for her, as some wounded men were to be put into the carriage. Mrs. Tyrrell's alarm now became excessive—she
looked

looked round for the person, who had consented to let her remain in the cabin, and getting her arms round him reminded him of his promise. He acknowledged his engagement, but confessed he had not power to perform it—that she must go with them, but would be accommodated with her own carriage. Three or four men then thrust her into the carriage, which moved on, attended by an immense body of people, and a great number of officers. When they had proceeded about a mile, the carriage was stopped and entered by Col. Perry, who said, he was fatigued. Mrs. Tyrrell endeavoured to prevail upon him to let her go—but in vain—she told him, she would use all her influence for his advantage, if ever she had an opportunity—He answered that the yeomen had taken a general officer, at Clonard, and that she must remain, a prisoner till his fate was known—After some time, the carriage was stopped again, and a fellow came in, who told Col. Perry, he had a right to it, as he had taken it, and tho' quite a common fellow, Perry had not power to prevent

vent him. Mrs. Tyrrell then applied to this man for protection; he anfwered, that fhe could not obtain her liberty. She was now reduced to all the anguifh of defpair, when a gleam of hope fuddenly darted acrofs her mind, upon feeing a man riding befide the carriage whofe countenance was perfectly familiar—This was one *Kearns*, a popifh prieft, who had been for fome time a curate in the neighbourhood of Clonard, and had always been received in Mr. Tyrrell's houfe, with the refpect due to his clerical function and the hofpitality of an Irifh gentleman. Upon meeting a man, who had feafted for weeks together at her table; and a clergyman too! fhe thought herfelf fecure, and implored his protection: he coldly anfwered—" O yes, Madam"—But with all the bafe and black ingratitude of a fullen and unfeeling heart, infenfible of paft kindnefs, he drew back his horfe, and with the jefuitical prevarication, natural to fuch a character, determined not to interfere, while he affected to confole her with an implied offer of affiftance——Thus deferted fhe again abandoned ed herself to despair, and began to prepare herself for that death, which she now looked upon as inevitable.——A man who sat upon the boot of the carriage, was suddenly struck with the fervency of her devotion, and turning round, said, *He* had as much authority as any other man there, and that the lady should do as she pleased. Elevated a little from her despondency by this expression, Mrs. Tyrrell gave him her gold watch, promising him any further reward he would demand, if he would procure her liberty——At this time a person in the garb of an officer, and whose countenance beamed with the rays of humanity rode up to the carriage—she immediately addressed him in the most supplicating terms—imploring him to take pity upon a poor defenceless woman, who had not, and who could not injure him—He interrogated her as to who she was and how she came there—She told him—He protested that he did not before know of any such thing, and requested to know what she wished to do——She replied that she only required to be let on her feet, that she might

proceed

proceed home. He immediately ordered the cavalcade to ſtop—handed her out of the carriage in the moſt kind and humane manner—conducted her thro' an immenſe crowd of armed men, and apologized for not accompanying her to Clonard, by ſaying, " ſhe knew he could not do it with ſafety."—Mrs. Tyrrell made him the acknowledgements of a grateful heart, and begged to be entruſted with his name, that if ever it ſhould be in her power, ſhe might return the kindneſs ſhe had then experienced, and repay the obligations ſhe had received.—He ſaid, he was afraid ſhe could not do him any ſervice, and with apparent reluctance told her, he was Captain *Byrne!*—He then returned to his party, and Mrs. Tyrrell having met ſome of the people in whoſe cabin ſhe was a priſoner, they accompanied her to Clonard, where ſhe was conſoled for all her ſufferings by finding her huſband and children alive.

The gentleman (for ſuch his conduct evinced him to be) who called himſelf Captain *Byrne*, proved to be Mr. *Byrne*, of Ballymanus, in the county of Wicklow, who afterwards ſurrendered himſelf

himself to Government, and Lieutenant Tyrrell being in Dublin at the time, repaired to the Castle, had an interview with Mr. Byrne, expressed his acknowledgments to him in the warmest terms, and represented the conduct of Mr. Byrne to the Administration in such a manner, as shewed the Lieutenant's sense of the obligation, while it promoted the lenient disposition which was afterwards manifested to Mr. Byrne.

Thus have we given an authentic detail of the battle of Clonard and the circumstances attending it, which in fact have been but little known, no official account having ever been published concerning it. One subject of regret however remains for the victors in the loss of Mr. Richard Allen, who died of his wounds a few days after at Mullingar, regretted by all who knew him, as a young gentleman of unsullied integrity and undaunted courage—attached to his King by the purest principles of loyalty, and to his family by the warmest affection—He was a zealous yeoman and a steady friend. All that seems necessary to add,

add, is to say a few words respecting the fate of this rebel army and its leaders.

### FATE OF THE REBELS.

After proceeding some distance from Clonard along the Dublin road, they turned to the right and took up their quarters for the night in the village of Carbery—where they possessed themselves of Lord Harberton's house, and indulged in drinking wine and spirits to excess—they were most of them intoxicated, in which state had they been attacked, they must have been totally destroyed—But the force at Clonard was too small, had suffered too severely, and expended too much ammunition to attempt a pursuit. On the morning of the 12th of July, the rebels moved from Carbery to Johnstown, and from thence by the Nineteen-mile house into the county of Meath—They were pursued by Lieutenant Colonel Gough, with a small party of the Limerick militia, and the Edenderry yeomen—An express had been sent to Col. Gordon, commanding at Trim, to march out with a force from thence, and co-operate with the Edenderry detachment—Col. Gordon

Gordon accordingly left Trim, with 200 men and two pieces of cannon, but from some ‖ fatality, yet unexplained, did not join the attack, which Lieutenant Col. Gough, after waiting some time and reconnoitring the enemy posted upon a hill, commenced against them, with only sixty infantry and twenty cavalry. The event of that engagement is well known, the rebels were completely defeated, leaving immense booty of cattle, &c. behind them.

They were next pursued by General Myers, with detachments of the * Dublin yeomenry, and Buckinhamshire militia, and tho' the General was not fortunate enough to overtake them, yet he drove them towards Slane, where they were attacked by General Meyrick, and in several subsequent days were met by different military bodies, who succefsively routed them, so that at length this formidable body was completely dispersed.

CHARACTER

‖ *The cause has been since fully explained to the Editor—See* PART *the* SECOND, *Page* 323.

* *Nothing respecting the Yeomenry of Dublin having appeared in this* NARRATIVE—*The Editor as-*
*sures*

## CHARACTER OF COL. PERRY, AND PRIEST KEARNS WHO WERE EXECUTED.

Every man who survived thought only of providing for his own safety.—Colonel *Perry* and Father *Kearns* made their escape into the King's county, and were attempting to cross a bog near *Clonbollogue,* where they were apprehended by Mr. Ridgeway and Mr. Robinson of the Edenderry yeomen, who brought them to that town, where they were tried and executed by martial law. *Perry* was extremely communicative, and while in custody both before and after trial gratified the enquiries of every person who spoke to him, and made such a favourable impression, that many regretted his fate—He acknowledged, that 150 of the rebels were killed and wounded at Clonard—which tho' accomplished by 27 men will not appear extraordinary, when it is known that these 27 men fired upwards of 1300 ball cartridge!

*Kearns* *sures that truly respectable body he has reserved for a future publication a variety of particulars respecting their* ALERTNESS *and unshaken* LOYALTY, *at a time when surrounded by imminent danger—to a great part of which the Editor (being then in their ranks) was an eye witness; how well they discharged their duty*

*Kearns* was exactly the reverse of his companion—he was silent and sulky, and seldom spoke, save to upbraid *Perry* for his candid acknowledgments—The history of this Priest is somewhat extraordinary—He had actually been hanged in Paris, during the reign of *Robespierre*, but being a large heavy man, the lamp-iron from which he was suspended, gave way, till his toes reached the ground—in this state, he was cut down by a physician, who had known him, brought him to his house, and recovered him. He afterwards made his escape into Ireland;— was constituted a curate of a chapel near Clonard, and having suffered so much by democratic rage and insurrectionary fury, he was looked upon as an acquisition in the neighbourhood, then much disturbed by the defenders—He inveighed against these nightly marauders with such appearance of sincerity and zeal, that he was frequently consulted by the magistrates, and sometimes accompanied them in their patroles—Some suspicion of treachery on his part was at length entertained,

from
*duty by guarding the Metropolis, so much the object of attack, and securing its internal quiet, will be remembered by every friend to the Constitution thro' future*

from the uniform difcovery of the operations agreed upon by the magiftrates, in confequence of which, he was excluded from their councils, and a pofitive information being fworn againft him for inftigating a murder which was afterwards actually committed, he fled into Wexford, where he became a member of an affaffinating committee, in which capacity he continued to be extremely active, until he accompanied Col. *Perry* upon the expedition into Kildare, which he is known to have encouraged, and which finally led him to that fate, which was the juft reward of an hypocritical and malignant heart, filled with gloomy and ferocious paffions—He feemed rather to be an inftrument of Hell, than a minifter of Heaven, for his mind was perpetually brooding over fanguinary fchemes and plans of rapine, while he affumed the facred veftments of a fervant of Chrift!

*The following Authentic Letters, carefully collected by the Editor, may be relied on, having been written by Persons of undoubted Veracity, who were fully assured of the facts therein recited.*

## LETTER I.

CARLOW, JUNE 31st, 1798.

*My dear Friend,*

YOUR affectionate letter I did not receive till eight days after date: I have felt much uneasiness at not having it in my power to answer it sooner; you may think it strange that in the space of ten days I could not procure time for that purpose, but were you acquainted with my situation you would be convinced that it is a fact. If I live to see you, I trust fully to convince you of the same.

Providentially for me I was absent from Carlow the time of the attack on that town—I say providentially; for my warm spirit and forward disposition might have led me into danger. The account which I received from people of veracity, who were on the spot is as follows.

On

On the 24th of May, the day preceding the attack, Haydon, a yeoman, but an officer of the rebels, repaired to the country, and spent the day in muſtering his forces. A letter relative to the buſineſs, directed to Mr. J. D. of Arles, was by miſtake put into the hands of a loyal yeoman of the ſame chriſtian and ſirname, and reſiding in the ſame place: the bearer was conveyed to Maryborough and executed, and the letter ſent to Col. M—— who commanded in Carlow, by means of which the miiitary had timely notice of the intentions of the rebels. There being no barrack for infantry in the town, the men were billeted upon the inhabitants: the genteeler ſort paying for their lodging, they were in general quartered in the cabins. The intention of the rebels was to murder the ſoldiers in their lodgings, ſurpriſe and take the Horſe Barracks, and then make themſelves maſters of the town, which in all probability they would have done, had not God brought their deſigns to light in the manner above mentioned; for on receipt of the above information the infantry were ordered

into

into the barracks, and kept under arms till the infurgents had entered the town.

About twelve o'clock the rebels came forward in great force; and too confident of a victory not yet gained, gave three cheers, crying " the town is our own!" but how dreadfully were they difappointed! for in that moment, the military rufhing forward, cut them down in all quarters; and having pofted themfelves in an advantageous manner, cut off almoft all poffibility of a retreat. Many of thefe deluded creatures fled into the houfes for fhelter; but there juftice purfued them—for the foldiers fet them on fire immediately. About eighty houfes were burned, but the numbers confumed therein could not be afcertained.

It is fuppofed not lefs than fix hundred fell that morning; and what is furprifing, only two I believe were found among the bodies with any fymptoms of life!

Thus did God fruftrate the defigns of the wicked, and difplay his juftice and mercy in a fingular manner.—His *juftice*, in fuffering the ungodly

ungodly to fall into the pit which they had digged for their innocent, unoffending neighbours; and his *mercy*, in preserving those whom he employed as the executioners of his vengeance on his enemies. Not a soldier or yeoman was so much as slightly wounded! One soldier indeed, who had not left his billet, they hung with a sheet; but being soon extricated, he recovered immediately.

Sir E. C. Bart. Haydon, Kelly, Kane, Borro, two Murphy's, one of them a Serjeant in the yeomenry, and several others were executed a few days after. Haydon, it is said, finding it going against his friends, slipt into his father's house, dressed himself in his regimentals, and came out and fought against those whom he had a few hours before led to the slaughter.

Thus by the interference of HIM who declares a hair of our head cannot fall without his permission, was an innocent people saved from the murderous designs of a sanguinary foe.

I remain yours affectionately,

F. R.

LETTER

## LETTER II.

Ross, July 20th, 1798.

*My dear Friend,*

The following account relative to the affair at Rofs is remarkably brief: particulars would fill a volume; and as there are many things faid concerning it which cannot be depended upon, I think it beft to confine myfelf to a few plain facts which are not difputed by any.

On the 4th of June in the evening, the rebels to the amount of near 20,000, took poffeffion of Corbit-hill, one mile diftant from Rofs. The military force in the town was remarkably fmall; the fears of the inhabitants were raifed to an alarming height, but the coming in of the county Dublin militia quieted them much.

Between three and four o'clock on the morning of the fifth, the engagement commenced. Early in the action the rebels were for fome time victorious, having driven before them all the black cattle they could collect through the country; this threw the military into confufion, and

obliged

obliged many of them to retreat in great diforder over the bridge; in confequence of which, fome pieces of cannon fell into the hands of the enemy. The rebels then fet fire to the houfes in the fuburbs, about two hundred and fifty of which were confumed; but this turned to their own difadvantage, for the wind blowing towards them, they were inveloped in fmoke, which, together with the immediate quantity of fpirituous liquors they drank on Corbet-hill, rendered them incapable of their bufinefs. The Dublin and Donegal militia, who kept the guards at the Market-houfe and Fair-gate, never left their poft, by means of which the rebels could not penetrate into the centre of the town; had they ran, Rofs, and in all probability the provincial towns in Munfter would have fallen.

The foldiers who retreated (except fome who fled to Waterford) foon rallied again, and entering the town in a furious manner, obliged the enemy to run. The battle lafted for near twelve hours!—3000 rebels, it is faid, lay dead in and near the town! Many alfo muft have died of their wounds;

wounds: 'tis thought that between fifty and sixty of the military fell: 'twas too many, but we could hardly expect such a victory on more reasonable terms. In this engagement Lord Mountjoy fell, also Col. Ladwell of the 5th dragoons, and Quarter-master Hay of the Mid-Lothian. Gen. Johnson upon whom the fate of this battle chiefly depended, had three horses killed under him, but he happily received no wound. B. B. Harvey was commander in chief of the rebels; but for his bad generalship on that day was deposed, and the command was afterwards given to Roach

It was on this dreadful day that the * barn at Scollabogue (in which one hundred and seventy Protestants, men, women, and children, were confined) was burned: the rebels in their retreat from Ross set it on fire, lest the prisoners should escape. About twenty of these sufferers I was personally acquainted with, some of them were my intimate friends. I pass within two miles of the melancholy spot every month, and often converse with those who know every particular relative to it, both loyalists and rebels.

Yours, F. R.

* *The reader is referred for all the particulars to pages* 291—300.

## LETTER III.

COLLIERY, AUGUST 1, 1798.

*My dear Friend,*

IT would give me much satisfaction to have it in my power fully to comply with your request, by furnishing you with an accurate detail of the engagements which took place between his Majesty's troops and the rebels, for the publication you mention. If the following particulars, to which I was an eye-witness can be of any service, you are at liberty to make what use you please of them.

On the morning of the 23d of June, 1798, the rebels, who had been driven from Vinegar-hill, appeared opposite New-bridge, or Gore's-bridge, a neat village on the river Barrow, county of Kilkenny. The forces quartered there, consisting of one troop of the 4th dragoon-guards, and a company of the Wexford militia, prepared to stop their progress, and in order thereto took possession of the bridge; but perceiving the rebels planting their cannon on the opposite side, and fording the river in confiderable numbers, (the water being low) they were obliged to retreat: all the cavalry efcaped, but about twenty of the infantry were made prifoners, many of whom were put to death on that and the following day. Their intention (as one who had been a prifoner with them informed me) was to form a junction with the colliers, and after taking Caftle-comber, to proceed to Kilkenny on Monday morning.

From New-bridge they proceeded through Kelly-mount (plundering as they went along), to a hill five miles from Caftle-comber, in the range of mountains called the Ridge, where they ſtopped for the night.

Finding it impoffible to get to Rofs, according to my travelling plan, I was obliged to take up my quarters in the colliery the week before. Here I remained in total ignorance of what was going forward in other parts of the country, till the twenty-third, the day above mentioned, when an exprefs arrived, informing us that the rebels had croffed the Barrow, and were on their

way

way here. In order to know the truth of the information I rode off, accompanied by a friend towards the Ridge. After riding about three miles I got in view of the rebel camp, and by the affiftance of a pocket telefcope could difcern their number to be about 8000. They had two ftand of white colours, and fome foldiers (I fuppofe thofe taken that morning) along with them; Here I met ten or twelve loyalifts with fire-arms; two or three of their company were juft murdered by the rebel picquets, and fome more wounded. Having procured a mufquet I advanced with four more till we came in fight of the dead bodies; but as the rebel fcouts were within mufquet fhot we did not think it prudent to venture farther.

Seeing a man covered with blood, a diftance from me, I called to him; he crawled forward and fell at my feet—he was a loyalift, and had received a dreadful wound from a broad fword on the head, and a few flight wounds on other parts of his body. Imagining there was no probability of his recovery, I advifed him to make the beft ufe of the few remaining moments he had,

had, but on examining his wounds, and having cauſe to believe they were not mortal, I bound them up in the beſt manner I could, and procuring a horſe to carry him, my friend and I, at the riſk of our lives, brought him four miles acroſs the mountains to Caſtle-comber, where his wounds were dreſſed: he is now perfectly recovered; and the happineſs which the remembrance of that tranſaction affords me, more than compenſates for the danger which attended it.

From ſeven till ten o'clock, the roads were crowded with the Proteſtants, flying from all parts of the adjacent country, into Caſtle-comber. At one o'clock a troop of the 4th dragoons, a company of the Downſhire militia, and a few yeomen, arrived from Ballinakill; theſe, with a troop of the Royal Iriſh dragoons, two companies of the Waterford militia, and one corps of yeomen cavalry, about two hundred and fifty in all, made up the whole of our military force; a ſmall number to oppoſe eight thouſand furies! but that the battle is not to the ſtrong, the event of that day proved.

About

About four o'clock the rebels arrived at Gurteen, three miles from Caftle-comber, where they heard mafs; at five they had mafs again, (it being a holyday), at the gizebo, a mile nearer.

Between fix and feven the engagement began at Cool-bawn, one mile and half from town. Being with the advanced guard, I was prefent at the commencement. The rebels advanced in the moft daring manner, and in pretty good order, having placed their mufqueteers in the front, who kept up a brifk fire. I continued behind the infantry for about fifteen minutes, during which time the balls were whiftling on every fide. I was fo ignorant as to enquire what occafioned the whiftling noife, and being informed it proceeded from the balls, I began to think of providing for my fafety, as my prefence there was ufelefs, having at this time no arms. I then planted myfelf behind the pier of a gate; but obferving the rebels advance and the foldiers to give way, I rode back to the town: the cavalry followed immediately, and juft behind me fhot a villain, who had the audacity to defire the officer to furrender the town. Here I had a miraculous efcape; for many of the infantry who came down clofe behind me were fhot, by lurking rebels from behind the hedges.

The military then took poffeffion of the bridge, where the battle continued hot for the fpace of fifteen minutes, when Captain G—n ordered a retreat: the cavalry, and part of the infantry inftantly obeyed; but about twenty of the Waterford militia abfolutely refufed, declaring " they would prefer death to difhonour." They were moftly Roman Catholics! I had not heard the orders, but my horfe taking head ran off; when I knew their intentions I did not attempt to prevent him. We halted about a mile and half from the town, when looking behind we beheld it all in a blaze; the rebel inhabitants, and fome who came the back way, fet it on fire. The firing ceafed for a few minutes, the caufe I know not, but words cannot exprefs what I felt in that moment: I concluded that my unoffending friends had fallen victims to the

rebel

rebel favages : they were prefented to my imagination in a thoufand dreadful forms. God pardon my feelings in that moment! How hard it is to forgive fuch enemies. I proceeded flowly till I met General Afgill, with about 1000 men : with thefe I returned, funk with forrow, fearing the tragic fight, which I expected to prefent itfelf on entering the town, would be too much to bear; but thanks be to God my fears were groundlefs—the few military which remained, and about thirty Proteftants, who were determined to fight for their wives and children, or perifh with them, kept poffeffion, nor fuffered a rebel to crofs the bridge. Our cannon, by miftake, played on the town for fome time, but providentially no lives were loft thereby. The rebels, on fight of the reinforcement, took fhelter in the woods, and from thence killed a few of the military; but eighteen rounds of grapefhot diflodged them. 'Twas four in the afternoon before they retreated. It is faid 400 of the rebels fell. There were twenty-fix Proteftants in coloured cloaths, and about twenty foldiers

killed,

killed; some of the former were butchered in cold blood, in a manner too dreadful to relate.

For the safety of Kilkenny, the troops were obliged to return there that night; the loyalists who fled with them, I think could not be less than six hundred; they left the most of their property behind them, which a party of the rebels who returned carried off.

The hand of God was visible in our deliverance that day; but remarkably so in three instances which I shall mention—*First*, from midnight till five o'clock, we had the greatest fog I remember to have seen; had it not been for this, in all probability the rebels would have divided themselves into different parties, and surrounded the town: but being strangers in the country, and not knowing where they might meet the army, they kept in a body on the main road, and attacked us but in one place. *Secondly*, the burning of the town; for the day being remarkably calm, the smoak lay on the street, which prevented them from seeing our force; for had they known that the army fled,

'tis

'tis more than probable they would have entered, as there were many entrances unguarded.

*Thirdly*, the Waterford militia's disobedience of orders—had they retreated, without a very extraordinary miracle, the loyalists would have fallen a prey to their unmerciful enemies.

Yours, &c. F. R.

## LETTER IV.

KILKENNY, AUGUST 30, 1798.

*My dear Friend*,

IN a former letter you have an account of the fate of Castle-comber, &c.—I have only to notice in this, that some gentlemen who fell into the hands of the rebels, while in possession of that town, were brought into the presence of the rebel General Murphy, who is said to have been a priest in the co. Wexford, and was excommunicated for his bad conduct many years ago.— He was dressed in black, affected the appearance of a stupid enthusiast, and shewed some bullets, which he said had been fired at him, but had rebounded from his invulnerable body—incredible as it may seem, this wretched invention was

generally

generally believed by the more wretched dupes under his command—You have here a real statement of the facts, of which I know you have sufficient curiosity to desire to be informed.

On Monday morning† our reconnoitering parties observed the rebel army posted on the bog, between John's-well mountains and the Ridge, about eight miles distant from this city—they seemed to be at rest, and remained quiet, except when relieving their centinels, till four o'clock, when they were observed to move to the right, along the Ridge, towards Kelly-mount and Newbridge.

In the course of the evening several false alarms electrified the inhabitants here—yet the garrison was left the whole day at rest. Next morning, Sir C. Asgill marched with a large force, consisting of two pieces of artillery, part of the Wexford and Wicklow regiments; of the 4th, 5th, and 9th dragoons; of Hompesch's cavalry, the Romney fencibles, and of the Kilkenny, Gowran, Fasiadineen, Shillelogher, Desart, Thomastown,

† *The writer omitted the date.*

Myshall

Myshall and Kellishin cavalry, he was joined on the march by the Leighlin-bridge infantry, and part of the Downshire militia, with their artillery, also the Maryborough and Ballyfin corps of yeomen-cavalry.

About six o'clock he came up with the rebel army, amounting to from five to six thousand men, advantageously posted on a rising ground, in an extensive flat, at Kilcomny, near Gore's-bridge—nothing could exceed the joy of our brave soldiers, after so many fatiguing marches, at last to have a pleasing prospect of retaliating; the officers were constantly obliged to restrain their ardour. The engagement began with a terrible fire af artillery, which the rebels returned with quickness, but entirely without effect.

A very hot fire was kept up near an hour, but unable to withstand the impetuosity of our troops, the rebels began to give way, and fled towards the county of Wexford.

A horrible slaughter now ensued, which lasted six or seven hours, nor did it cease while a rebel was to be seen—1100 rebels were left dead on the

the field of action! among whom was the *invulnerable commander, Murphy*. This victory was so very decisive, that we got possession of all their artillery, amounting to fifteen pieces, of different calibre—all their standards, ammunition, and baggage, a vast number of pikes, musquets, swords, &c. seven hundred horses, a great quantity of black cattle, sheep, &c. also a vast quantity of bedding, blanketting, and wearing apparel, which were given up to the soldiers who bravely contended for the same.——Yours, &c. &c.—

## LETTER V.

MARYBOROUGH, APRIL 20, 1799.

*My dear Friend,*

BEING desirous of making public the valour of the troops of this town, &c. under the command of Major Matthews of the Royal Downshire regiment, against the rebels, I send you a plain narrative of facts as follows:

On the 24th of June, 1798, four hundred of the Downshire regiment, with their battalion guns, Captain Pole, with the Ballyfin troop of yeomen-cavalry, and Captain Gore, with the

Maryborough.

Maryborough, (both troops under the immediate command of Captain Pole) proceeded towards the collieries of Caftlecomber and Donane, by order of Sir Charles Afgill. On the road we faw Caftle-comber on fire; foon after we arrived at Moyad, and faw the rebel army in great force on the high grounds above Donane; we then received intelligence that Sir Charles had engaged them at Caftle-comber that morning, and that his force was at leaft double ours, but that he had retired to Kilkenny. It was now too late in the evening for us to attack; we therefore fell back on Timahoe, determined to engage them in the morning. At Timahoe an exprefs met us from Sir Charles, defiring we fhould return to Maryborough; this was anfwered by an exprefs from us, propofing to Sir Charles to attack the rebels next morning on the road from Donane, and that we would attack on the road from Timahoe. The anfwer to this propofal we received at feven o'clock next morning from Sir Charles, who would not agree to it, as he faid his troops were fatigued, but left it to us to fight, if we could

could do it with fecurity, where we were, or to return to Maryborough. We chofe to rifque the former, and the proper arrangements being made, returned to Moyad, where we had laft feen the rebels: when our cavalry arrived there they found the rebels had gone off to the Ridge; where we purfued them, and were again difappointed in bringing them to action, as they had marched for Gore's-bridge: our cavalry then proceeded to Old Leighlin, from which place Captain Pole, who had gone forward for intelligence, fent an exprefs to inform Sir Charles Afgill of what he had done, and of our intention to attack the rebels wherever we found them. At Old Leighlin we met with Mr. Vigars, to whom our intention of attacking the rebels was made known, and he, feeing our troops much fatigued, immediately fupplied us with a number of cars to carry them, without which affiftance we fhould have been much diftreffed; he likewife accompanied us to the fcene of action, and was always in front giving us every affiftance in his power. The whole corps arrived at Leighlin-bridge
about

about twelve at night. In two hours after an express came from Sir Charles, desiring us to meet him at Gore's-bridge, at five in the morning; we instantly marched, but on the road we got such intelligence as induced our commanding-officer to alter his route, in order to get between the rebels and the mountains; an account of which he sent to Sir Charles, by Mr. Moore, collector of this place, who, with his brother, Mr. Pierce Moore, marched with us, and to whose able advice and knowledge of the country, I heard Major Matthews say, we in a great measure owed our success. After a march of about three hours we came in sight of the rebels; and as soon as we got sufficiently near, fired some cannon shot at them: they retired from us about a mile and a half to form their line; we followed in column, with our guns in front, and our cavalry in the rere; just as we got orders to form our line for the attack, we heard Sir Charles's cannon on the other side of the hill; at this instant our cavalry were ordered to charge, which they did in a most gallant stile; the rebel line was inftantly broke, and we joined Sir Charles's troops in the purfuit, which continued with great flaughter for above fix miles; all the cannon, horfes, ftores and prifoners they had were taken, and their army difperfed.

When it is known that the rebel army would not have been brought to action, or even an attempt made upon them, but for the exertion of this little corps—and when it is known that this corps purfued a large body of rebels, at leaft five thoufand ftrong, with ten pieces of cannon, for nearly forty miles, without orders or directions from any general officer whatfoever, and that, except fome bread they got at Leighlinbridge, not a man of them tafted food for forty-four hours, I think you will agree with me that they did their duty, and that their country ought to know it.

Yours, &c. &c.——

LETTER.

## LETTER VI.

BELFAST, APRIL 29, 1799.

Sir,

IN compliance with your requeſt I ſhall ſet down briefly what has been already communicated to the public; but muſt, through the medium of your intended publication, be more generally circulated.

On Saturday morning, June the 9th, 1798, Colonel Stapleton having received intimation of a number of people aſſembled at Saintfield, and neighbourhood, he ſet out from Newtownards, with a detachment of the York fencible regiment, accompanied by the Newtownards and Comber yeomen cavalry and infantry; altogether about 320 men, and two field-pieces.

About half paſt four o'clock in the evening, this little army fell in with a body of rebels, ſuppoſed to be between ſix and ſeven thouſand men, near Saintfield!

The light infantry, commanded by Captain Chetwynd, advanced with great gallantry, to ſecure an eminence on the right, which having accompliſhed,

accomplished, he was attacked by a force of at least three thousand rebels—the front armed with pikes, the centre and rear with musquets, whose fire galled them severely, till the body of the troops and field-pieces came up, when the rebels were routed with huge slaughter. The rebels, by their own account, lost above five hundred men, among whom were many of their leaders. The King's troops, after routing the insurgents, marched to Comber, where they halted during the night—next morning proceeded to this town.

I am much concerned to inform you of the loss of three brave officers by those miscreants hands in this action—Captain Chetwynd, Lieut. Unite, and Ensign J. Sparks: Lieut. Edenson was wounded. The whole return of the killed and wounded of his Majesty's troops were—29 killed, and 22 wounded. The valour of the officers that fell in this engagement, deserves to be publicly recorded, but that of the amiable, gallant, and much-beloved Capt. C. ought not to be passed without particular notice.—This brave
fellow,

fellow, at the head of his men, received no less than nine pike wounds! notwithstanding which, he continued his position, encouraging by his example his men to fight like loyal soldiers; till alas, two wounds from musquets deprived this hero of his existence, and our country of his future services.

Poor Sparks—whose race of glory was now ended, was but sixteen years old, and had just before he fell, received for his intrepid conduct the public approbation of his commanding officer.

Too much praise cannot be given the Newtownards and Comber yeomen-cavalry, who, conducted by Capts. Houghton and Cleland, evinced the greatest intrepidity during the whole of the action.

If it be possible to convince those deluded creatures, who were then in arms against the peace and prosperity of this nation, (and of their certain destruction, should they again have recourse to such rebellious measures,) it must be the event of the above action, where so many were cut off by such an inferior force.

P. S

P. S. It was ludicrous to behold the varied badges of diſtinction as worn by the rebel chiefs; ſome were dreſſed in green jackets, turned up with white, others yellow; white veſts, buck-ſkin breeches, half-boots, hats with white cock-neck feathers and green cockades, &c.

Yours, &c.——

## LETTER VII.

TYRELL's-PASS, APRIL 30, 1799.

*Dear Friend,*

I SHOULD have anſwered your favour ſooner, but was making every poſſible enquiry in order to furniſh you with the beſt account of the engagement at Kilbeggan. The gentleman, the bearer of this (one of our officers), and I, were preſent on the occaſion.

On the 17th of June 1798, (on the preceding day a fair was held in Kilbeggan. The lower order of the people appeared uncommonly civil, and this country had a more placid appearance than for ſome time before) at 11 o'clock at night, a recruit of Capt. Clarke's, gave information that the town would be attacked on the next day. As many similar alarms had been circulated before, this was not much regarded—however, the videts of horse were ordered to keep a sharp look-out, and give instant intelligence, should any number of men be descried by them.

At break of day (at that time of the year about two o'clock), some persons were perceived on the top of a hill westward of the town. Immediate notice of this was given to the officer commanding, who directed that the horse-guard should continue to observe the motions of the enemy; and should their numbers encrease, to retreat slowly, about two hundred yards in front to the town, and apprize him of the same.

It soon appeared that their force was between three and four thousand, divided into bands, from sixty to an hundred, in regular order, with different kinds of arms, principally pikes, from five to ten feet long, pitch-forks, &c. Each band moved separately, headed by an officer, distinguished by a green sash or cockade—most of the men had white paper bands round their hats.

It

It was generally remarked that they had all clean fhirts on, had each a piece of oat-bread in their pockets, and many were apparently intoxicated.

The town (the fubject of this letter) has not been remarkable for loyalty—the principal fears of the garrifon arofe from an apprehenfion of treachery. There were then under arms fixty of the Northumberland fencibles, about thirty of the Fertullagh cavalry, and thirty loyal Proteftants, who either belonged to the town or had fled there for refuge.

On the firft appearance of the rebels, (three hours before the attack commenced, (an exprefs was fent to Tullamore, where the principal part of the 7th dragoons lay—General Dunne forwarded a troop, about eighty in number— the want of a fufficient force was of the worft confequence, as the rebels attacked our party in the mountains, and obliged the fencibles to retreat back to the town—Meantime the loyalifts cleared the ftreets, which were now full of rebels without the loss of a man—the cavalry pursued—Serjeant Price alone killed fourteen pike-men. On hearing the firing a few of the cavalry stationed at Tyrrell's-pass flew to the scene of action, just before the Black-horse arrived—both, aided by the dismounted from Tyrrell's-pass killed 400 of the enemy.

Yours, &c. C. F.

---

The Publisher having waited in vain for a detail of the engagements at ‖ Naas, Kilcullen, Hacketstown, &c. and public curiosity daily encreasing, being desirous of gratifying the same, he deems it most advisable to insert the following OFFICIAL ACCOUNTS received at the Castle.

*Extract of a Letter from Lord Viscount Gosford, Colonel of the Armagh Militia, and Major Wardle, of the Ancient British Light Dragoons, to Lieutenant General Lake, dated Naas, Thursday Morning, 8 o'Clock, 24th May, 1798.*

This morning, about half past 2 o'C" Dragoon, from an out-post, came in at

‖ *Those battles have come to hand, and are give in* PART *the* SECOND.

formed Major Wardle, of the Ancient British, that a very confiderable armed body were approaching rapidly upon the Town. The whole garrifon were inftantly under arms, and took up their pofition according to a plan previoufly formed in cafe of fuch an event happening. They made the attack upon our Troops, pofted near the goal, with great violence, but were repulfed: They then made a general attack in almoft every direction, as they had got poffeffion of almoft every avenue into the town. They continued to engage the troops for near three quarters of an hour, when they gave way, and fled on all fides. The cavalry immediately took advantage of their confufion, charged in almoft every direction, and killed a great number of them. A great quantity of arms and pikes were taken, and within this half hour many hundred more were brought in, found in pits near the town, together with three men with green cockades, all of whom were hanged in the public ftreet. We took another prifoner whom we have fpared, in confequence of his having given us information that will enable us to pursue these rebels; and from this man we learn that they were above a Thousand strong: They were commanded, as this man informs us, by Michael Reynolds, who was well mounted, and dressed in yeoman uniform, but unfortunately made his escape; his horse we have got.

About thirty rebels were killed in the streets; in the fields, we imagine, above an hundred; their bodies have not yet been brought together.

It is impossible to say too much of the cavalry and infantry; their conduct was exemplary throughout.

*Extract of a Letter from Lieutenant General Dundas to Lord Viscount Castlereagh, dated Naas, May 25th, 1798.*

IN addition to the account which I had the honor of sending you yesterday, I have the satisfaction to inform your Lordship, that about 2 P. M. yesterday I marched out again to attack the rebels, who had assembled in great force on the North fide of the Liffey, and were advancing towards Kilcullen-bridge: They occupied the hills on the left of the road leading to Dublin; the road itfelf and the fields highly enclofed, on the right. The attack began between 3 and 4; was made with great gallantry, the infantry forcing the enemy on the road, and driving them from the hills on the left; the cavalry with equal fuccefs, cutting off their retreat. The affair ended foon after 4. The flaughter was confiderable for fuch an action; one hundred and thirty lay dead. No prifoners.

I have the further fatisfaction of ftating to your Lordfhip, that his Majefty's troops did not fuffer in either killed or wounded. The rebels left great quantities of all kinds of arms behind them, and fled in all directions.

This morning all is in perfect quietnefs. General Wilford, from Kildare, joined me laft night; an officer with whom I ferve with unfpeakable fatisfaction.

The troops of every defcription, both officers and men, fhewed a degree of gallantry which

it

it was difficult to reſtrain within prudent bounds —Captain La Touche's corps of yeomenry diſtinguiſhed themſelves in a high ſtile.

***

*Extract of a Letter from the Rev. James M<sup>c</sup> Ghee, Vicar of Clonmore, Co. Carlow, dated Hacket's-town, three o'Clock, P. M. May 25, 1798.*

IN conſequence of an information received this morning, that a large body of rebels were marching to attack the town, Lieutenant Gardiner, with the men under his command, and a party of yeomenry commanded by Captain Hardy went out to meet them. Having reconnoitred their force, which amounted to between three and four thouſand, they took poſt on a hill under the church, and when the rebels came tolerably near, the officers and men made a feint and retreated into the barrack.

The rebels ſeeing this, came on with a great ſhout, immagining the day to be their own. In a few minutes Captain Hume came up with about thirty of his troop, and inſtantly charged them,

‡ *For the ſecond attack on Hacket's-town, ſee* PART *the* SECOND *page* 185.

on which the rebels retreated. A general purfuit took place; and fo complete was the rout that above three hundred of the mifcreants now lie dead on the field of battle.

To fay that the *Antrim* regiment behaved well is not any thing new ; but the yeomen under Captain Hardy's command behaved aftonifhingly ; nor can I fufficiently commend the conduct of Captain Hume and his corps; for though his right arm was in a fling, owing to a very fevere fall from his horfe, which prevented his ufing his fword, he headed his men with gallantry, and went on with fpirit and bravery that furprifed every one confidering his fituation.

As to Lieutenant Gardiner, his conduct and fteadinefs throughout the whole affair is far beyond my praife; but I am forry to inform you that a fevere blow of a ftone he received on his breaft from a villain whofe life he had juft faved, prevents his writing to you himfelf. He is however, thank God, walking about, and having been let blood is much better ; the villain was fhot dead on the fpot.

Every

Every one of the *Antrims* was vying with each other who should do his duty best; and I have very great pleasure in telling you that not a man (Lieut. Gardiner excepted, and one soldier, who received a contusion in his arm) was in the least injured.—In short the loyalty and zeal of the whole party was beyond any thing that has been seen on a similar occasion.

---

The Publisher having been favoured with the two following letters by an intimate friend, (to whom they were written without any intention of appearing in print,) and also being personally acquainted with the writer, assures the Public that every particular set forth may be received as Facts.

Such is the established character of the writer, (as known to numbers,) that he would not advance a falsehood—he was in most engagements from the breaking out of the late rebellion to the defeat of the French at Balinamuck; an account of which is now in the possession of the Publisher, and given in the *Second Part*.

LETTER

## LETTER VIII.

Some account of the battle of Arklow, by W. H. G. of the Armagh militia, in a letter to a friend in Dublin, dated Arklow, June 13th, 1798.——Written on the field of action.

*My dear Friend,*

I wrote to Mr. H. by one of the conductors, who promised to leave the letter at your house, in which I gave him a circumstantial account ‡ of what took place from the time I left Naas, till the battle of Gorey, and our retreat to Wicklow afterwards.

On Saturday last we were informed that the rebels in great force were pursuing us: the drums beat to arms, and our forces assembled immediately. Our general formed a square of infantry at one end of the town, and left the cavalry to defend the other. In a little time

‡ *This account has come to hand, and is given in* PART *the* SECOND, *pages* 120—4.

the

the out-posts were driven in, and shortly after appeared their colours flying. They extended for more than five miles around us: a most awful sight! In order to intimidate us they fixed their hats on their pikes and rushed on.

Their artillery were placed on an eminence which commanded us—Their armed men in front, and pike to charge in the rere. In this order of battle they came forward. We waited the first onset: in a few minutes the firing commenced in all quarters, which lasted from four o'clock in the afternoon, till near nine at night. They endeavoured to break our square in every quarter, but like true soldiers we cleaved together and repelled them; they stormed our little line twice, but were beat back with slaughter; they drove their dismounted horses to the mouths of the cannon in order to shelter themselves, but the grape shot made them fall on every side; they even set the town on fire in order to annoy us with the smoak, but the wind at the order of *our God* turned, drove it from us and confounded them in their own device; they

did

did every thing like inveterate enemies, and defperate madmen to accomplish their ends; and their priests informed them that they could catch the Heretics balls in their hands, and threw some (as tho' they had caught them) to their rebellious mob to fire again at us, and declared they could beat us with the dust of the earth. Oh what superstition! This was confirmed by deserters from their camp, who informed us likewise, that flushed with victory at Gorey, they thought that after they had taken Arklow, nothing could stop them till they arrived at Dublin; and indeed I believe that this battle for the present, has decided the fate of this Kingdom.

One of the Antrim militia, who fled from them after the battle reports their army to have been 20,000 strong. Among the slain was Father Murphy * from the County of Wexford. They lost about 1000 killed and wounded, and numbers were hanged in the streets. Every regiment vied with each other for victory; we took several stand of colours from them, made of green, white and yellow stuff. We have pre-

* *There were several of this name.*    pared

pared every thing in cafe of another attempt—
If they do not come forward, we will go immediately and retake Gorey, and ftorm their camp. They are greatly difcouraged. Bleffed be God, notwithftanding I was expofed to a heavy fire, I never received one wound. On our fide we had about 18 killed and 28 wounded. We are all in high fpirits. Captain Knox of the yeomenry, and two of his men, were killed purfuing the rebels. Our men, in a former engagement, kept the town of Gorey, when the reft of the army left them. They are worth gold. Pardon this fcroll, as I am in hafte. We have been under arms thefe four days and nights.

   Farewell,

     I am yours, W. H. G.

*A minute account of this battle will be hereafter given.*

## LETTER IX.

GOREY CAMP, JUNE 28, 1798.

*My dear Friend,*

A deliverance from hoftilities and fevere fatigue, thefe two days paft, affords me an opportunity

tunity to address you. In my two last letters to Dublin, I gave a particular account of those facts to which I was an eye-witness—You shall now have those which have since occurred.

The 13th inst. we received orders to move forward from Arklow, and in the evening arrived at Gorey—but oh, what a strange reverse! The town, in the absence of the army, was plundered, and almost totally destroyed by the rebels; even the church did not escape their sacrilegious fury!—they demolished the windows, dragged down the pulpit, and tore to pieces many of the pews; but what is still more shocking to relate, at which your soul must recoil, stained it with the blood of two Protestants, whom they immolated inside—they burned the two elegant seats belonging to the Ram family here.

The rebels, upon being apprised of our approach, broke up their camp, and precipitately retreated to Vinegar-hill.—We next morning pursued, and killed several of them on the way. In the evening we pitched our tents in a small village

village called Houlet, within seven miles of Wexford, with an intention of remaining there for the night; but perceiving their pickets on an adjacent hill, that commanded our camp, at ten o'clock we struck our tents, marched by a circuitous route, and in the morning, at dawn of day, we found ourselves on the off-side of their daring position.

From their great numbers and strong bulwarks they concluded they were impregnable. It is allowed they had that day on Vinegar-hill 30,000! We reconnoitred for some time, and distinctly observed them to draw up in *solid lines*. The battle, by the command of General Lake, was to commence at nine o'clock. His army took one side of the hill to bombard it, the light brigade, under Colonel Campbell, took another—other commanders were fixed in like manner. Our brigade, consisting of the Armagh, Cavan, Durham, Antrim, and part of the Londonderry, Dunbarton, Tyrone and Suffolk—in all about 3000 brave troops, had to march four miles; it being appointed that we should flank them in another quarter. I shall

I shall give you a view of their situation—Vinegar-hill * is very steep, rising in the form of a cone: at the but of it are two other hills, with quicksets and other ditches across them—these were lined with their musquetry men:—a river runs at the bottom of both, and adjacent is a small wood. At the bottom of Vinegar-hill is the once beautiful, but now ruined town of Enniscorthy—on the top of the great hill is the but of an old windmill, on which they had placed their *green flag* of defiance—in a word, the position of the rebels was one of the strongest I ever saw. The rebels did not wait the time appointed, but commenced cannonading at seven o'clock. They could not tell what to make of the bombs, and said, " They spit fire at us."—Indeed they answered the desired end, by the numbers they destroyed upon their bursting.

The light brigade, assisted by the cavalry, gained one of the lesser hills, planted their cannon, and played briskly on them: in a short time we possessed ourselves of both—the rebels made to the top of Vinegar-hill with all possible

\* *The Editor has an excellent View of this Hill and Battle engraving, which will be shortly published.*

speed

speed—the soldiers pursued hard after them, and beat them off it. In a little time the *green flag* became a prey to the Royal Band, who triumphed in its fall—it was an arduous attempt, but we succeeded in the end. The rebel commanders deserted their men when they found the day proved unfavourable to their interests and fled towards Wexford, leaving the deluded wretches to be cut in pieces.* The engagement lasted two hours and an half—the soldiers merited the cloth they wore, and gloried in the name of WILLIAM. Our brigade remained all night in the demesne of Harvey Hay, one of the rebel chiefs: next day we returned to Houlet again, where we encamped for two days: the scouting parties killed more after the different engagements than what fell in battle—many of their commanders were taken and hanged. We have suffered much from lying on the roads and ditches rolled in our blankets. I have almost lost my hearing, but am content when the *good old cause* triumphs.

* *There were only 16 Rank and File killed, and 62 wounded, of his Majesty's troops in this Engagement.*

At Vinegar-hill we killed men of seventy years old—we rescued three officers of the Antrim militia, and twelve privates of the same regiment: yesterday we hanged two of them for endeavouring to vote away the lives of two of the above officers and soldiers when prisoners.

Yours truly,<br>W. H. G.

---

The following letter was written by a sufferer in the Wexford rebellion, while in possession of the rebels—it fully corroborates the truth of the atrocities stated in the Narrative by Charles Jackson, printed (to bind with this Work,) and now selling by the Publisher hereof.—price 6dh.

## LETTER X.

WEXFORD, May 1st, 1799.

Sir,

Altho' I have not the happiness of being personally acquainted with you, at the request of your friend, Mr. W—s, it affords me pleasure to have it in my power to send you a copy of an *accurate detail* of the effects of the late dreadful rebellion,

rebellion, as it respected this part of the Kingdom, written by an intimate and fellow sufferer with me, and transmitted to Dublin, for publication in July 1798.

On Friday evening the 25th of May, 1798, about nine o'clock, the North Cork militia, then quartered here, with the Wexford yeomen cavalry and infantry were ordered under arms, in consequence of an alarm that the Insurgents were rising in the neighbourhood of Camolin, in this county; and we continued under arms the whole of that night. On Saturday orders arrived here from Dublin Castle to the high sheriff, to apprehend B. B. Harvey, J. Colclough of Ballyteigue, and Edward Fitzgerald of New-park; and they were committed to goal on Saturday evening and Sunday morning. Early on Sunday morning the 27th of May, an express arrived here, that the day before an engagement took place between a party of the Camolin cavalry, commanded by Lieutenant Buckey, and a large body of the rebels; that the Lieutenant was killed, but that they had repulsed the rebels; that they were then (Sunday morning) in great force in the neighbourhood of Oulart, burning the houses of different Protestant inhabitants in that part of the county. In consequence of this information; Lieutenant Colonel Foote, with Major Lombard, and six other officers, and 106 men of the North Cork militia, immediately proceeded from this town, and came up with the rebels at an advantageous position they had taken on a hill near Oulart. § Through the rashness of the Major, in charging the rebels in an incautious manner, the whole party were surrounded and not a man escaped instant destruction but the Lieutenant Colonel and two privates. By this defeat the rebels had acquired a powerful accession of strength and confidence; having got the whole of the arms and about 57 rounds of ball-cartridge from each man, they not having fired above three or four rounds when they attempted to charge them with Bayonets. On the following morning, the 28th, the rebels attacked Enniscorthy, and after a severe conflict of three hours, and above 500 of them being

§ *Accounted for*, PART *the* SECOND *page* 99. slain,

slain, they took it, owing to the treachery of some of the inhabitants in setting fire to the town during the engagement, which obliged the militia and yeomenry to § evacuate it; and they, with all the loyal inhabitants that could escape, retired on Monday evening to Wexford. On Tuesday the 29th, the rebels formed two powerful camps, one at Vinegar-hill, near Enniscorthy, and the other about three miles from Wexford at the Three Rocks, on the road between Wexford and Ross, and sent threats in here that 10,000 men would be detached from those camps to attack the town next morning.—On Wednesday the 30th, information was received that a body of the military, (supposed to be the 13th regiment) was attacked by the rebels near their camp at the Three Rocks; this induced Lieut. Col. Maxwell, who arrived the day before with two hundred of the Donegal militia, to march out with his men and four troops of yeomen cavalry to their assistance; but before he had come up with them, they entirely cut off the party, which proved to be a flight detachment

§ *Further particulars are given in* PART *the* SECOND, *pages* 102—8 of the Meath militia, of about 100 men, who were coming to Wexford with three howitzers; and with thefe howitzers the rebels attacked Col. Maxwell's party, and obliged him to retreat into Wexford. The 13th regiment, who were coming to our relief, finding they could not proceed to us without attacking the rebel camp, returned back to Waterford. From thefe rapid fucceffes, and their encreafing numbers, as it was fuppofed there were then 20,000 men ready to attack Wexford the people here were panic-ftruck; and finding that many who were entrufted with arms had deferted their colours, and it being confidered that others could not be depended on, the officers concluded that the town was not tenable, and without firing a fhot it was evacuated on the 30th of May, and fhortly after entered by the rebels, who kept poffeffion of it until the 21ft of June. As to the different engagements the army has had with the rebels at Rofs, Newtown-barry, Arklow, &c. you muft already be informed of them; in many inftances the reports were vague and contradictory, I fhall therefore

therefore confine myself to such particulars as fell within my own knowledge, or that I have reason to believe are facts.

The atrocities committed by these ferocious tygers while they held this town, were I believe unprecedented. After taking poffeffion of the town without oppofition, they immediately fhot feveral Proteftant inhabitants, tore open moft of our houfes, deftroyed and carried off our effects: their (rage was moft particularly directed againft poor Mr. Daniels and mine,) put every Proteftant inhabitant whom they fpared from immediate death (fome few excepted that they received amongft them) to prifon; but they would not ftop here, we were obliged to flaughter each other. The Sunday after they had taken the town, June the third, Pigott, Robfon, a Mr. Edwards and I, were dragged from our cells, and forced by the rebels to put to death a man for being an approver againft a prieft of the name of Dixon, who had attempted to fwear him to be an United Irifhman; after being made the inftrument of his deftruction, we were forced to to drag his body from the place of execution and throw it into the river. After deliberating for some time whether they should difpatch us at that moment or not, they carried us back to goal. Others of the prifoners were obliged to perform the like office to another approver. After every fpecies of infult and tyranny to us in prifon, the fatal day at length arrived, (Wednefday the 20th of June!) when the total extermination of the prifoners (namely 500) and all the Proteftant inhabitants of the town, man, woman and child, was openly avowed to be their fixed purpofe! About 95 of the prifoners were taken out and tortured to death by pikes, on the bridge of Wexford; they returned for more victims, and I was dragged out of the cell, when above fifty wretches (whofe ill will I had incurred by exerting myfelf in the line of my duty,) cried out to have me deftroyed. Providentially an exprefs arrived at that moment, that the army had defeated a confiderable party of the rebels at Long Graige, between this and Rofs, and requiring an immediate reinforcement;

this

this made them beat to arms, and induced them at that time to stop the work of blood. The following day they were totally defeated at their great camp (as they termed it) at Vinegar-hill, and routed in all directions, and on the same day the remaining prisoners were liberated by the army. The horrid cruelties, they committed in this town fell short (if possible) of what they did in other parts of the county; at Scullabogue, between Taghmon and Ross, they put 150 Protestants into a barn and burnt them to death; amongst whom were two beautiful and accomplished young ladies of the neighbourhood: poor G—d, the Surveyor of Taghmon, attempted to escape from the flames at this place and was shot by them—at Enniscorthy they scarcely left a loyal man alive that they could find, and the town was almost consumed by fire—There were about ten of their leaders hanged here, upon the arrival of the army, amongst whom were B. B. Harvey, Cor. Grogan of Johnstown, Captain Keughe, J. H. Colclough of Ballyteigue, and Kelly of Killan, who were afterwards beheaded,

and

( 86 )

and their heads placed over the Court-house. In consequence of a proclamation from General Lake, inviting the rebels to desert their leaders, and promising pardon, numbers came in with pikes, &c.——

Such my dear Sir, is the recital of what I can recollect of the barbarities practised here during the reign of these monsters. What my feelings and sufferings were during that period, I cannot attempt to describe. That the Almighty providence may preserve us all from such another visitation, is the ardent prayer of, Yours, &c.——
*The following Clergymen and Gentlemen, were taken Prisoners and put to death by the rebels.*

The Rev. Samuel Haydon, Enniscorthy; Rev. Robt. Burrowes and ‖ Son, Oulart; Rev. Francis Turner, Ballingale; Rev. Mr. Pentland, Killan; Rev. Mr. Troke, Templeshambo; Captain Allen Cox, Coolelife; Major William Hore, Harpurstown; Edward Turner, Esq. Slaney Lodge; Edward Howlin D' Arcey, Esq. Dalnahown.

‖ *This Gentleman tho' perforated has happily survived!*

APPENDIX.

# APPENDIX.

NO account having appeared of the attack at Prosperous, 'tis presumed the following AFFIDAVIT made before the Right Hon. the Lord Mayor of the City of Dublin, will furnish the reader with most particulars relative thereto. The Examinant is well known to the Publisher, and favoured him with a copy of the same for the present *Narrative*. The Examinant suffered much in the rebellion, being obliged to desert his house and property to a considerable amount, which became a prey to the rebels.

*County of the City of Dublin, to wit.* } The examination of T. D. late of Prosperous in the County of Kildare, who being duly sworn on the Holy Evangelists, maketh oath and saith; That for many nights previous to the night of the 23d of May last, this examinant and his family were very much alarmed lest they should be attacked by the rebels commonly called United Irishmen.

That examinant thought he and his family were in fome degree fecure, by the arrival of detachments of the Ancient Britons and the North Cork militia; That however examinant ftill continued to be alarmed, as his houfe was a confiderable diftance from the barracks; That examinant faith that he was awakened about the hour of one o'clock in the forenoon, by the barking of a large dog he had, and fome time after he was alarmed by the firing of fome fhots; examinant faith that on looking out of his window, he perceived a great body of people armed with pikes and fire-arms, between whom and the foldiers in the barracks a conftant firing was maintained; That as the balls paffed by this examinant's houfe, and one of them clofe to his head, he withdrew and let down the window; That foon after examinant faw the barracks on fire, and heard the foldiers exclaim, " The houfe is on fire"; we fhall be burnt up or fuffocated, we can fight no longer." That foon after examinant faw the roof of faid barracks fall in; examinant faith that the faid rebels (whofe numbers

bers had encreased so much as to fill the streets of Prosperous, and to cover the adjacent fields) on the falling of the roof of said barracks, gave many shouts, which seemed to rend the skies, and made this examinant and his family thrill with horror; That the said rebels exclaimed, " That the day was their own, and they would there plant the Tree of Liberty." Examinant saith that the said rebels knocked at his door, and desired to have it opened, expecting to find there a party of soldiers who had been billeted there a short time before, and Mr. Stamer, who had lodged therein when he went there to receive his rents,—part of the town of Prosperous belonged to the said Stamer; examinant saith that the said rebels approached his house in a large body, six of whom preceded the rest mounted on some of the horses which they had taken that morning from the Ancient Britons at Prosperous; that examinant as soon as he came out of his door, was surrounded by a party of the said rebels who presented their pikes at him, and who he expected, from the ferocity of their looks would

would have inftantly put him to death; that one of the faid rebels held a mufquet at examinant's breaft with his finger on the trigger; that another of the faid rebels who was a turf-cutter, held a drawn fword over examinant's head; and examinant verily believes they would have inftantly put him to death, but a young man in the crowd who feemed to have fome influence interpofed, beat down the mufquet which was prefented at his breaft and faid he fhould not kill him; examinant faith that he knew many of the faid rebels, to whom he and his family had been very kind. That foon after the faid rebels went in queft of the faid Stamer, who lodged at fome diftance from the faid town; that having feized him the faid Stamer, they led him through the ftreet by examinant's houfe, furrounded by a number of pike-men, while a low fellow held a piftol at his head; examinant faith that as he paffed by the examinant's houfe, he the faid Stamer caft a melancholy farewel look at examinant and his family,—that foon after the faid rebels maffacred the faid Stamer. Examinant faith that foon after

he

he went out with an intention of enquiring for his friend Mr.———an inhabitant of Profperous, and that before examinant had gone far he was again furrounded by the faid rebels, who, he verily believes would have put him to death, but for the interference of the perfon that had faved him before ; examinant faith, he difcovered foon after that Mr. Brewer, a refpectable manufacturer of faid town, who had employed many of the faid rebels, had been maffacred by them, and that his body had been mangled with favage barbarity; examinant faith that they alfo maffacred a poor old man of the age or 70 years and upwards, who ferved as Serjeant in his Majefty's forces, they having confidered him as an Orange-man ; examinant is convinced in his mind the only reafon why the faid rebels murdered the faid Serjeant was his being a proteftant ; examinant faith that when the faid rebels had committed the faid barbarities, they exclaimed with favage joy " where are the Heretics now? fhew us the face " of an Orange-man"; examinant faith that many women, who acting with the faid rebels,

ufed

used expressions of that nature, as often and as loud as the men, and that some old women who were amongst them seemed to brighten on the occasion, and to shew as much fervent joy as the youngest amongst them. That some of the said women kissed and congratulated their fathers, their husbands, or their brothers, on the victory they had gained, and exclaimed " Dublin and Naas have been taken and are in possession of our friends; down with the Heretics, and down with the Orange-men." Examinant saith that many of the wretches who had been actors in that bloody scene, had come into the town of Prosperous the preceding day, and in presence of Capt. Swayne, of the North Cork militia, who, with a party of his regiment that morning, viz. the 24th of May, they had massacred, and also in the presence of their parish priest, of the name of Higgins, and declared their contrition for their past errors, and gave the strongest assurance of their loyalty for the future—that many of the said rebels surrendered their pikes to the said Swayne, and as such surrender was considered as a test of their repentance,

repentance, and as neceffary to entitle them to written protections, numbers of them lamented that they could not obtain fuch protections, as they never faw nor had a pike, and that many of them declared they would fell their cow to purchafe a pike if they knew where it could be bought; examinant faith that notwithftanding thefe declarations many of the faid rebels appeared in the ranks well armed with pikes; examinant faith he is convinced in his mind that the faid rebels would have plundered and burnt all the other loyal houfes of Profperous, and would have murdered the remaining proteftant inhabitants thereof, but that a party of the Ancient Britons and the Cork militia, being a part of the detachment they had murdered that morning, unexpectedly approached the town, and that the faid rebels on their appearance, fled towards the bogs and morraffes; examinant faith he could not refrain from fhedding tears at feeing fuch fcenes of favage barbarity, and that a fervant who continued faithful to him defired him not to fhew any fign of concern, left he might draw on him the anger and vengeance of the rebels. (*A true Copy.*)

END OF PART FIRST.

# BY AUTHORITY.

## *IN THE PRESS,*

to be printed on Wove Paper, and published in a few Days by the Printer hereof—price 2s. 8dh.

### THE
### *JOURNAL*

of a distinguished Personage, particularising every interesting occurrence relative to the *French Invasion*, during their stay at KILLALA, &c.

This Production, coming from the pen of so respectable a Character cannot fail of exciting and fully gratifying public Curiosity.

---

## *A NEW EDITION OF*
## CHARLES JACKSON

(*Being the Fifth*)—Price 6dh.

Giving an Account of his Sufferings and Providential Escape from the Wexford Rebels, to be had at all the Booksellers where JONES's NARRATIVE is Sold.

# AN IMPARTIAL NARRATIVE

OF THE MOST IMPORTANT

# ENGAGEMENTS

WHICH TOOK PLACE BETWEEN

## HIS MAJESTY'S FORCES

AND THE

# REBELS,

DURING

# The Irish Rebellion,

*1798.*

INCLUDING VERY INTERESTING INFORMATION
NOT BEFORE MADE PUBLIC.

---

CAREFULLY COLLECTED
## FROM AUTHENTIC LETTERS.

---

Embellished with Engravings of the Battles of Arklow and Tara-Hill.

PART II.

DUBLIN:
Printed and Sold by John Jones,
91, BRIDE-STREET.

1799.

(Price 3s. 3d.)

TO THE

# Yeomen of Ireland.

*My Lords and Gentlemen,*

THE Loyalty, Courage and Patriotism which proved the Salvation of *Ireland* point you out as the proper PATRONS of this little Work. It is Dedicated to your Service, and will prove, I should hope, not undeserving of your Protection. When REBELLION, with all its savage Horrors, tarnished the Irish Nation, and spread Desolation thro' the Land, you rallied

rallied round the sacred Banner of your KING and CONSTITUTION, and preserved your Country, at once from Infamy and Destruction. The following RECORD of your glorious Atchievements is the Effort of an humble Individual and zealous Friend to your Institution, anxious to perpetuate the memory of your Virtues. Relying on the purity of his Intention, but feeling his inadequacy to the execution of the Design, he throws himself upon your Indulgence, and subscribes himself with the utmost respect,

      Your Faithful and
          Obedient Servant,

Public Printing-Office,
91, Bride-street.
November 4th, 1799.

          *J. JONES.*

# PREFACE.

THE FIRST PART of this WORK met with such flattering Succefs (paffing through three EDITIONS in four MONTHS,) as encouraged the Editor to ufe every poffible Exertion to complete the SECOND—He devoted his Time in acquiring new fources of CORRESPONDENCE, and collecting MATTER for the enfuing PAGES. The generous offer of Affiftance from numerous Gentlemen, who patronized the WORK, was gratefully accepted, and feveral Favours thus tranfmitted are given in their original Form. Enriched with the elegance of polifhed Diction, the Editor faw no room for Emendation, and he became apprehenfive that any attempt to alter might injure, when it could not improve. The ftate of Affairs in the NORTH and the tranfactions in LONGFORD and CAVAN will be found highly interefting.—Some Accounts indeed are detailed in the unadorned Style of the

Soldier, but it is the expreffion of Sincerity; the language of the heart! and while its fimplicity forms a pleafing variety, contrafted with other parts of the Work, the Reader is gratified with the intrinfic Evidence of its TRUTH.

A very great proportion of this Work will therefore be found to confift of original NARRATIVES: Some Official DOCUMENTS have been introduced, partly with a view of fupplying a Defect, and partly for the purpofe of confirming what might otherwife appear Doubtful; the Editor being anxious upon every occafion to fhew his adherence to his firft principle, AUTHENTICITY.

He feels very fenfibly that a NARRATIVE of FACTS in the order of time in which they happened would be more fatisfactory; this however was impoffible, as many Particulars were communicated after a great part of the Work was at Prefs; but in order to remedy this

# PREFACE. vii

this as much as possible, a *Chronological Table* is annexed, which will enable the Reader to trace each ENGAGEMENT which took place from the breaking out of the REBELLION to the Defeat of the FRENCH.

The different Manuscripts received have been carefully filed, and some Gentlemen, whose situation gave them superior opportunities of local Knowledge, have perused the Sheets after they were printed, and when any material Error was discovered, the part was cancelled at no inconsiderable expence;—the Editor sacrificing his Interest to his solicitude for Correctness. This circumstance occasioned the *Supplementary Pages* and *Errata*, which being thus accounted for, it is hoped the Reader will excuse.

Deeply impressed with a sense of the Importance of this Publication, he regrets that his Situation did not enable him to do it more justice; but full of confidence in the candour of the Public, he commits the Product of his humble Efforts to their kind and generous Protection.

*DIRECTIONS TO THE BINDER.*

BATTLE OF ARKLOW, to face page 70.
BATTLE OF TARA, to face page 161.

|  | Page. |
|---|---|
| Circumstantial account of the Battle of Oulart, | 98 |
| Battle of Enniscorthy, | 101 |
| The town evacuated by the loyalists, who retreat to Wexford, | 107 |
| Battle of Ballycanow | 109 |
| Battle of Ovit's-town, | 113 |
| Battle of Antrim, | 116 |
| Death of the Rt. Hon. Lord O'Neil, | 119 |
| Battle of Tubbernerneen near Gorey, | 121 |
| Death of Col. Walpole, | 122 |
| King's Troops are defeated | 123 |
| Battle of Ballymore, | 125 |
| Battle of Kilculler, | 128 |
| Death of Captains Cooke and Erskine, | ib. |
| Four hundred and sixty rebels killed, | 131 |
| The loyalists evacuate Kilcullen (which is entered by the rebels,) and retreat to Naas, | ib. |
| Perkins the rebel commander's terms to General Dundas, | 135 |
| Lord Jocelyn's Fox-hunters kill 350 rebels on the Curragh of Kildare, | 137 |
| Rev. Mr. Williamson's providential escape, | 138 |
| Quarter-master King barbarously murdered at the rebel camp | 139 |
| Battle of Monastereven | ib. |
| Battle of Newtown Barry | 144 |

(a) *Lieut.*

## CONTENTS.

| | Page |
|---|---|
| Lieut. Col. O'Reilly's account of the Battle of Ballynafcarty, | 149 |
| General Lake's account of the retaking of Wexford, | 151 |
| The rebels terms to, and Gen. Lake's anfwer, | 153 |
| General Moore's account of the battle at Gough's Bridge, &c. | 154 |
| Expreffes relative to the rifing in the Co. Meath, | 157 |
| Rev. Mr. Nelfon and Mr. Kellet murdered, | 160 |
| Battle of Tara, | 162 |
| Affairs of the North, | 169 |
| Rebels defeated at Randul's-town, | 175 |
| General Nugent's account of the battle of Ballynahinch, | 179 |
| Battle of Kilcavan-hill, | 187 |
| Battle of Hacket's-town, | 189 |
| Death of Captain Hardy, | 190 |
| Rev. Mr. Magee and three good Markfmen kill and beat off hundreds of the rebels, | ib. |
| Heroic conduct of Mrs. and Mifs Fenton, | 192 |
| The loyalifts retreat from Hacket's-town to Tullow, | 192 |
| Battle of Rathangan, | 195 |
| Captains Spencer and Moore, with eighteen Proteftants are maffacred, | 196 |
| Attack at the Rev. Mr. Whitty's Providence, | 197 |
| French Invafion and fecond Infurrection, | 200 |
| Poem on the French Invafion | 20 |
| Particulars of the affairs of Killala during the Invafion, | 20 |

# CONTENTS.

| | Page. |
|---|---|
| General Trench's account of the retaking of Killala, | 208 |
| Gen. Humbert's letter to the Bishop of Killala, | 212 |
| Copy of a very minute Journal of the Battles of Castlebar, | 214 |
| French and rebels commit great depredations, | 220 |
| Teeling and priest Kean prevent the massacre of the Protestants, | 221 |
| Humbert's proclamation, | ib. |
| —pompous letter to the Directory, | 223 |
| —letter to the French Minister of Marine, | 227 |
| Defeat of the King's troops at Castlebar accounted for, | 230 |
| The French leave Castlebar, | 233 |
| Second attack by the rebels on Castlebar, | 235 |
| Captain Urquhart's wisdom in this battle—he is victorious, | 237 |
| Rebellion in the counties of Cavan, Longford, and Westmeath traced to its origin, | 239 |
| Names of the rebel commanders, | 242 |
| Indefensible state of Granard previous to its being attacked, | 243 |
| Captain Cottingham's elegant account to Lord Castlereagh of the memorable battle of Granard, | 245 |
| More particulars relative to said battle, | 250 |
| Situation of the rebels previous to the battle of Wilson's-hospital, | 253 |

(a2) Battle

# CONTENTS.

| | Page. |
|---|---|
| Battle of Wilson's-hospital. | 258 |
| Col. Vereker's account of the battle of Coloony | 264 |
| Gen. Nugent's approbation of Col. Vereker's conduct, | 268 |
| The Sheriff and Grand Jury of the Co. Sligo's thanks to Col. Vereker | 269 |
| Progress of the grand army destined against the French | 270 |
| Providential detention of the French at Cloon, | 274 |
| Defeat of the French, | 276 |
| Solemn thanksgiving held at Killishandra, | 278 |
| Gen. Lake's account of the battle of Ballinamuck, | 280 |
| Treachery of the French, | 281 |
| General Cradock is wounded, | ib. |
| Gen. Humbert's account to the Directory of his surrender, | 284 |
| Encomiums on the victorious army—on Lord Roden, &c. | 285 |
| Lord Cornwallis's letter to the Duke of Portland relative to the defeat of the French, | 286 |
| —approbation of the conduct of the army and yeomenry, | 289 |
| Mr. Grandy's affidavit | 291 |
| Describes the cruel conduct of the rebels at Scollabogue Barn, &c. | 292 |
| Father Murphy's harangues, | 294 |
| Evidence against Phelim Fardy found guilty of murder committed at Scollabogue, | 296 |
| Authentic account of the rebel atrocities at Vinegar-hill, &c. | 301 |

## CONTENTS.

|  | Page. |
|---|---|
| Confession of James Beaghan previous to his being executed on Vinegar-hill, | 304 |
| Joshua Chase (aged 80) charged with being an Orangeman, narrowly escapes death, | 307 |
| Conduct of William Byrne of Ballymanus, | 308 |
| —gives liberty to murder children, | 310 |

### SUPPLEMENT.

|  | |
|---|---|
| Circumstantial account of the murder of Lieut. Bookey, and fate of the murderers, | ib. |
| Tinehaly burned by the rebels, | 312 |
| Lord Roden defeats the rebels at Rosbawn-hill, | 313 |
| Ancient Britons surrounded near Carnew, | 315 |
| Rebels determine to murder the Protestants of Carnew, | 316 |
| —Are defeated and Carnew saved, | 317 |
| Names of Persons piked by the rebels | ib. |
| Battle of Ballyrahine-hill, | 318 |
| Anecdote of the celebrated Bridget Dolan, | 319 |
| Battle of Kilthomas, | 321 |
| Attack upon Leixlip, | 322 |
| Col. Gordon pursues the rebels from Longwood to Kilmullen, | 323 |
| Additional Particulars relative to the Second Attack on Hacket's-town, | 325 |
| Rev. Mr. Brownrigg animates the exhausted Army, | ib. |
| Rejects Mrs. Perry's proposal, | 329 |
| Chronological Table, | 327 |
| An Erratta, | 329 |

## TO THE EDITOR.

Sir,

I HAVE seen some sheets of the work which you are about to publish, and wish much (if it were practicable) you should contradict a passage in page one hundred and ninety-two, line nineteen, which charges the rebels on their retreat from Hacket's-town, with first ‖ *butchering all they met with, men, women, and children.* This is certainly contrary to the truth; as through the whole of that disastrous day, they treated the *women* † and *children* with humanity, sending them (as they fled from their burning houses) to places of safety and protection; and from first to last offering them no injury. In the favour of truth, you have my permission to make what use you please of this.

I am, Sir,<br>Your humble servant,<br>THEOBALD BROWNRIGG.

Mr. JONES, *Bride-street.*

‖ *The Editor produced to the Rev. Mr. B. his correspondent's* manuscript *of the particulars at Hacket's-town, and has, since the receipt of this letter, been respectably informed, that those only who were found wearing emblems of loyalty,* orange ribbons, lillies, *&c. became victims to rebel fury.*

† *See a corroborating testimony Pages* 325—6.

A NAR-

# NARRATIVE

## OF THE MOST IMPORTANT

# ENGAGEMENTS,

DURING

# The Irish Rebellion,

1798.

---

### PART II.

SOON after the twenty-third of May, large bodies of insurgents shewed themselves, and began to commit horrid outrages in the neighbourhood of Newtown-Barry, Ferns, and Enniscorthy, burning houses, and murdering many respectable persons. The military force in the county of Wexford was but small, the principal part of it composing the garrison of Wexford, which was the head-quarters of the North-Cork militia, under the command of Lieutenant-colonel Foot.

The garrison of Enniscorthy was commanded by Captain Snowe, of said regiment, and consisted of one company of the North-Cork, one company of Enniscorthy infantry (Captain Joshua Pounden's), and one troop of Enniscorthy cavalry (Captain Solomon Richards's); there was also a small detachment of the North-Cork at Ferns, and the Scarewalsh infantry, under the command of Captain Cornock. In consequence of a partial advantage obtained by the rebels in an affair near Ferns, in which Lieutenant Buckey, of the Camolin cavalry, was unfortunately killed, their numbers increased to an amazing degree; and their murders, burnings, and devastations, were carried on with a still more savage fury; the night served but to shew more distinctly the conflagration all around, and in the day-time the crowd of miserable sufferers flying in a state of distraction into the towns for shelter, impressed the mind with the utmost horror. In this situation the troops were employed on the most fatiguing duty; unable, from the insufficiency of their numbers, to have a relief during the night-time, and of course obliged to keep their whole force continually under arms till morning.

### BATTLE OF OULART.

On the ensuing morning, Whit-Sunday, the twenty-seventh of May, a body of the rebels, of about

ufand men, took poſt on the hill of
n eight miles of Wexford; of which
lonel Foott received immediate in-
m Mr. Turner, a magiſtrate of the
brought the intelligence himſelf.
nt-colonel loſt no time in ordering
inſtantly under arms, to march out
is banditti; and he determined to
himſelf. The detachment ordered,
ne hundred and ten men, including
ned officers, with Major Lombard,
: Courcy, and four ſubaltern offi-
arched off the parade in the higheſt
he idea of being the firſt to quell
ſurrection. When he had marched
iles, Lieutenant-colonel Foott per-
of rebels, as he ſuppoſed amounting
ur and five thouſand men, poſted
f Oulart, the ditches alſo of the
in their front, were lined with ſuch
as were ſupplied with fire-arms:
halted the detachment on the road,
pencil wrote a note on a ſcrap of
ſed to the officer he had left in
Wexford, requiring an immediate
—this note he ſent by the trumpeter
Hunte's yeomenry corps of cavalry,

*mer account, ſee* PART *the* FIRST,

sixteen or seventeen of which had joined the North-Cork on the march. By some fatality or other, which has never yet been accounted for, the detachment was moved from the road whilst the Lieutenant-colonel was writing this note, and a party of a serjeant and twelve men detached to endeavour if possible to take the rebels in flank, whilst the remainder of the detachment pushed forward, crying out that they would beat the rebels out of the fields; by this movement it was instantly engaged with the rebels, who fired upon it from behind the ditches; but the troops soon beat them from these, and they retreated taking similar positions behind others, from which they were also routed with much loss. This advanced party then fled in great disorder to the hill, where the main body, chiefly pikemen, were posted; and was pursued, in equal disorder, by the unfortunate North-Cork, whose impetuosity could not be restrained, although every exertion was used by the Lieutenant-colonel to prevent it. At this critical moment, the main body of the rebels rushed down from the hill in a swarm, surrounded the dispersed detachment, and piked every man in a space of time hardly credible; the Lieutenant-colonel, one serjeant, and two privates alone escaping. Lieutenant-colonel Foott was wounded in the breast by a pike, and nearly dragged off his horse, but being capitally mounted, he he galloped off the ground, clearing every ditch in his way; the serjeant who had been the one detached in flank, shot one of the rebels who was mounted, and by taking his horse made his own escape—how the two privates got off cannot be ascertained. Feats of great desperacy were performed by the ill-fated victims that perished; the grenadiers in particular, who having wrested their pikes out of the hands of several of their assailants, at last fell from blows and stabs behind.

The next day, Whit-Monday, the twenty-eighth of May, the rebels increased in numbers, to more than double, and supplied with the arms and ammunition they had taken from the unfortunate detachment, which had gone out with sixty rounds per man, and very few rounds of which had been expended, marched to Enniscorthy in the fullest confidence; they were commanded by General Roche, who had been permanent serjeant in Colonel le Hunte's yeomenry, and by father John Murphy, a Roman-Catholic priest. However, Enniscorthy had been reinforced the day before, by the detachment of the North-Cork and Captain Cornock's Scarewalsh yeomanry falling back from Ferns, unable to oppose the multitudes of rebels assembled in that quarter; the whole of the combined force now amounting to about three hundred men, under the command of Captain Snowe, and together with the loyal Ferns and Enniscorthy inhabitants, every man at his post, in the best positions that the situation and force would admit of.

## BATTLE OF ENNISCORTHY.

At one o'clock in the afternoon, the action commenced, by a vigorous attack made by the rebels on the Duffrey-gate side of the town, having previously turned in before them a great number of loose horses to confuse and disconcert the troops; at the same time, the ditches in front of the Duffrey-gate were lined with several hundred of their best marksmen, who kept up a galling fire: the attack was opposed by the yeomenry and loyal inhabitants with the greatest gallantry, but from the vast superiority of the rebel numbers, there was much danger of the yeomenry corps being surrounded—several loyal and brave fellows had fallen, amongst the rest Captain John Pounden, who commanded his brother's supplementary yeomen; but intelligence of it arriving to Captain Snowe, who was posted on the bridge, he marched up the whole of the North-Cork to their assistance. Just as he got to the Duffrey-gate, he was met by an officer of cavalry, and informed that it was necessary he should file off to the left, to prevent the intention of the rebels of surrounding the yeomenry,

by

by entering a road called the Daffney-road, which would have brought them into the town in the rear of them; this he accordingly did, and took a position on that road, where a rebel column was within a very short distance of him; but instead of attacking him, the rebels detached a large body to cross the river, which was very low, and to occupy the other side of the town (Templeshannon) and the bridge which he had quitted; by which means, had it succeeded, the troops of all descriptions would have been completely hemmed in; but the North-Cork ran back through the streets as quick as possible, to repossess the bridge, in doing which they lost a serjeant and a private by shots from the windows: however, they arrived critically in time to line the bridge, and to give a severe check to the rebel column, just then in the act of crossing the river, and a part of which had landed on an island in it. Numbers of the rebels fell upon this occasion, by the fire of the North-Cork from the battlements of the bridge; and none of their shots took effect from their confusion, from the protection of the battlements, and from most of them levelling so high, that their shot went whistling over the heads of the North-Cork, whose fire was so incessant, that it was with the utmost difficulty it could be restrained, even after the rebels had got beyond its effect. Another
body

body of the rebels had by this time made good a landing lower down the river, but an officer and sixteen men of the North-Cork was detached from the bridge, through Templeshannon, to meet them. The officer (Lieutenant Brien) now in the regiment, but then only acting as a volunteer, an old officer of the line, took an excellent position, by lining the ditch of a ploughed field, from whence, by the report made by him to Captain Snowe on his return, the rebels sustained no small loss.

Baffled then in their first attempt, the rebels ceased any further attack for at least a quarter of an hour, or twenty minutes, which gave Captain Snowe an opportunity of renewing the ammunition of his own men, which was almost all expended, and of sending a fresh supply to the yeomenry; he was enabled to do this, from having a car on the bridge with him with his ammunition-chest on it: in the mean time, the houses all around, on each side of the river, began to blaze, and exhibited a most awful spectacle. The rebels took immediate advantage of this, to make a second and most desperate attack on the Duffrey-gate and through the Irish street, and to send across the river to the Templeshannon side another body, much lower down than where they had attempted it before, in order to take the troops on both their flanks. Their numbers

bers and impetuosity were so great on the Duffrey-gate and Irish-street, that all the corps of yeomenry and the loyalists were obliged to retreat fighting into the very centre of the town, where they made a most determined stand:—and here they were opportunely and nobly supported by the fire of a detachment of one serjeant, one corporal, and fourteen privates, composed equally of the militia and yeomenry, under the command of serjeant Bennett of the Enniscorthy infantry. This detachment had been posted in the morning, in the windows of the court-house, which commanded the market-place, under the idea of what now really came to pass; and the execution from its fire amongst the crowd of rebels was dreadful—no shot missing. At this moment, Captain Cornock, wounded from the thrust of a pike along his neck, ran down to the bridge, to inform Captain Snowe of what was passing, and to request a reinforcement from the North-Cork, which was immediately complied with; Captain Snowe reserving no officer, and only one serjeant and sixteen rank and file with himself. This reinforcement had not been gone five minutes, when the rebels appeared in Templeshannon, at the opposite end of the street, fronting the party of the North-Cork, which had been drawn across that part of the bridge to oppose them; after exchanging two or three shots, the party advanced

rapidly

rapidly through the street with fixed bayonets and ported arms, finding nothing else for it, and apprehensive that a much larger body of rebels might come on: they met no opposition till they came to the brewery, when about forty men dashed in amongst them from a lane on their left, and an obstinate contest ensued hand to hand; but the North-Cork being all ready loaded, and their arms in the best order, succeeded in almost totally destroying this party of rebels, very few individuals saving themselves by flight: a small number of them only had fire-arms, but the pikemen, wonderfully tall stout able fellows, fought with their pikes in the most furious and desperate manner, thrusting at the soldiers, who had much ado to parry with their bayonets after having fired, before they could load again—out of the sixteen men, two were killed and one wounded in this affair. Previous to the reinforcement under Captain Joshua Pounden coming over from the Duffrey-gate, the formidable attack in that quarter had been repulsed by the united militia and yeomenry, and the great column of rebels completely driven out of the town. This happy success enabled Captain Pounden to march his corps immediately over to Templeshannon, to the assistance of Captain Snowe and his small party.

Notwithstanding

Notwithstanding the many repulses the rebels had received, in this very severe action of more than three hour's continuance, yet they had not drawn off; they occupied all the hills about Enniscorthy, and were seen in thousands climbing up the steep wood below the bridge, to take post on the road leading to Wexford—they well knew that the troops, exhausted with the constant duty they had underwent for several days and nights previous to the action, and with the day's action itself, were in no condition to oppose fresh and repeated attacks that would be made on them in the night; they had no cannon, and were inclosed in a burning town, without the possibility of getting any kind of refreshment. From a conviction of the truth of this situation, a retreat to Wexford was proposed to Captain Snowe, by the river instead of the great road, the town being no longer tenable; to which he at last yielded, after giving his opinion, that he did not know how far he might be justified in doing so; but being told that if he did not, his retreat would be entirely cut off in less than ten minutes, he ordered the drum to beat. The militia, yeomenry and loyalists marched off together, through the burning streets, the houses on each side of which were some blazing, others a cake of red fire; they carried off with them such of their wounded as were at all able to move, the yeomen cavalry

cavalry vying with each other which should give most assistance to these unfortunate sufferers, and equally so to the women and children, numbers of whom, inhabitants of Enniscorthy, followed the troops. No pursuit was attempted by the rebels, nor did they enter Enniscorthy for some time after the troops had evacuated it. In this day's action, Captain John Pounden, Lieutenant Carden, an old officer, and Lieutenant Hunt, fell; the latter at first only wounded, but afterwards murdered by the rebels, and about seventy of the troops, mostly yeomenry; several loyalists were also killed and wounded, on whose bravery too much praise cannot be bestowed. The rebels, by every subsequent account, lost five hundred men—they paid dear; for General Roche afterwards declared they were the flower of his army of fifteen thousand men, ten thousand of whom were armed with fire-arms and pikes, the remainder with such weapons as they could procure; however, their exact strength could not be ascertained, they were supposed by the troops in the action to be about ten thousand. Roche was mounted on a grey horse, wore a cocked hat, was dressed in scarlet, and had a drawn sword in his hand. The troops made good their retreat, and marched into Wexford that night by nine o'clock, in perfect order, both cavalry and infantry.

LETTER

## LETTER XI.

Ferns, Co. Wexford, June 22, 1799.

Sir,

A late publication of yours, entitled " An impartial Narrative of the most important Engagements which took place between his Majesty's Forces and the Rebels, during the Irish Rebellion, 1798," has just fell into my hands, and to do you justice, it must prove an acceptable publication, and a work of great merit. There is one engagement however, among many others, of which you have taken no notice, that is, the battle at Ballycanow, in this county, fought on Friday the first of June, 1798, of which I will endeavour to give you the particulars, being an eye-witness to the whole.

On the morning of the first of June, 1798, a party of the Camolin cavalry, consisting of an officer and about twenty men, were ordered by Lieutenant Elliot of the Antrim militia, on a reconnoitering party towards Corrigrua-hill, and to return to Gorey by Ballycanow. The party immediately marched, and on coming within sight of the hill, the rebels (who arrived there that morning from Vinegar-hill) had taken post on the summit, and in a few minutes kindled a large fire, as a signal for their piquet guards to come

come in. This somewhat alarmed us, as we were badly prepared with either arms or ammunition; but being determined, if possible, to obey our orders, we took another direction, and got to the crosses of Ballymore, where we saw a large party of rebels on the hill, and another party after setting fire to all the Protestant houses in the neighbourhood. Between this and Ballycanow a large party of the rebels were seen on their march from Oulart, being armed with guns and pikes, and a great variety of standards; on seeing us they hastened on to Ballycanow, thinking to cut off our retreat to Gorey, whilst the entire body from Corrigrua-hill were pouring down after us. Arriving at Ballycanow, a guard of rebels attacked us, which we defeated, without any loss on our side, except one man and his horse slightly wounded. On our going in to Gorey, we informed the Commanding-officer of these circumstances, and also that we were led to think their determination was to attack the town that evening or the following morning. Lieutenant Elliot thought it best to march his men out, meet the rebels, and not give them time to make a formal attack. Having ordered the drums to beat to arms, in about ten minutes the forces in Gorey, consisting of 20 Antrim, 20 North Cork, 20 Gorey Infantry, 50 Gorey cavalry, 36 Ballaghkeene cavalry, and 46 Camolin cavalry,

cavalry, marched out in high spirits to attack them.

## BATTLE OF BALLYCANOW.

On coming to the summit of Balymanane-hill, two miles from Gorey, and midway between that and Ballycannow, we had a full view of the rebel force: they had formed a camp in a plain field near the latter place, and were at that time refreshing themselves after their march. We proceeded down the hill, and within a mile distant of Ballycannow, the enemy had formed behind the ditches, whilst a large body marched towards us, driving horses and black cattle before them, for the purpose of throwing our troops into confusion. The action now commenced, which for an hour was very smart, when they were, however forced to give way, and fled with great precipitation; though they repeatedly attempted to form again behind the ditches, they were at last totally dispersed, with considerable loss. The cavalry pursued them in all directions, over a vast extent of the country; the infantry proceeded to Ballycannow, met with a rebel commander and commissary named Kenny, took him prisoner, and finding him guilty, shot him, and burnt his house, which contained property to a large amount. Two of the Gorey cavalry, and some loyalists who were made prisoners some days before, and doomed to suffer death that evening, were fortunately released by our troops, and by every account we could learn from them, their numbers were 1000 strong; that it was their intention to encamp on Ballymanane-hill that night, and to have attacked Gorey at an early hour the following morning; but it pleased God that they were frustrated in that particular. They also informed us that Priest Murphy (who was since killed at Arklow) had the command of the body, and that he blessed their pikes and guns, said mass for them, &c. in Ballycannow, before the battle began. We have been informed that their loss was not short of 200 killed, besides many wounded: their guns, pikes, standards and an immense number of horses mules and asses fell into our hands, while on the contrary we had no lives lost. Lieut. Elliot received a slight wound of a pike in the forehead, one of his men a wound in the thigh, and one of the Gorey troop wounded in the arm.

I remain, Sir,
Your Obedient,
Humble Servant,
P. C.

LETTER

## LETTER XII.

ROSBOROUGH, JULY 1ſt, 1799.

*Sir,*

I am only this day favoured with your letter of the 22d, Inſt. In anſwer to which, I beg leave to ſay, that Mr. M—ll has been under ſome miſtake as to my having any particular knowledge of theſe affairs with the rebels which you mention, except that on the 19th of June 1798, at Ovitſtown—which having been very briefly given in the Official Accounts from the Caſtle, I ſhall endeavour to ſtate ſome of the particulars, as well as in my power at this diſtance of time.

On the 18th of June 1798, Lieutenant Col. Irwine (having then the command of the garriſon at Trim,) received intelligence that a conſiderable body of rebels, were aſſembling in the neighbourhood of Kilcock, under the command of William Aylmer, formerly an officer in the Kildare Militia, and other leaders.—On that night about ten o'Clock, he marched with what troops he thought could be ſpared from the garriſon of Trim, and its vicinity, conſiſting of the following corps—viz. 4th Dragoon Guards, one troop; Duke of York's R. F. Highlanders, four Companies, and two battalion guns; Trim cavalry, one troop, Navan and Murgallion, one troop;

Demiſou

Demifou one troop; Trim infantry, one company: total in the field, 284 rank and file, with a due proportion of officers and serjeants.

Having paſſed through Kilcock, on the morning of the 18th, without ſeeing any rebels, or getting any intelligence to be depended on: about ten o'Clock the advanced guard was fired on by part of a lage body of them (by certain accounts ſince obtained from parties concerned; there was upwards of five thouſand) drawn up at the bottom of Ovitſtown hill, near Hortland houſe. It being ſome time before the detachments could be formed, owing to the the nature of the ground and the hedges, the rebels kept up a very ſmart fire, and made a deſperate attempt on the Guns in our front, though receiving their fire. Theſe deſperadoes however ſuffered for their temerity, by a conſiderable carnage, which ſoon made them abandon that favourite object.—They afterwards filed off to their right under cover of a hedge, with a view of ſurrounding the King's Troops, but in this they were alſo diſappointed, by our cutting through the hedge and falling on their flank, which completely routed them in that quarter—the difficulty of forming, being ſurmounted with the greateſt ſteadineſs by the troops, the whole body of rebels then gave way, and fled with the greateſt ſpeed to the neighbouring bog; where, by throwing away their arms and

and cloaths, they effected their escape, leaving dead on the ground upwards of two hundred.

The loss on our side was as follows, 4th Dragoon Guards, one Serjeant killed; Capt. Sir Richard Steele, one Serjeant, two Rank and File wounded; Murgallion Cavalry, one Rank and File wounded; Trim Cavalry, one Rank and File wounded; Duke of York's Highlanders, Ensign John Sutter, one Serjeant, and five Rank and File killed; Lt. Col. Irwine, one Serjeant, and seven Rank and File wounded,—the first slightly.

I have heard Col. Irwine say he received great assistance from Col. Burrowes of Dangan, (Co. Meath) who did him the honor to accompany us as a volunteer on the occasion, and that every individual of the detachments behaviour in this little Skirmish, was such as did them the greatest honor.

The above is a hasty sketch of the business agreeable to your wishes, which if thought worthy of mention in your publication, I assure you may be relied on as perfectly correct.

I am Sir,
    Your Obedient Servant,
        H. K.
LETTER

## LETTER XIII.

ANTRIM, JULY 12th, 1799.

Sir,

I this day (for the first time) had the pleasure of reading your very interesting Narrative, and not seeing any account of the battle fought with the rebels in this town, I take the liberty of giving you an account of that affair; though the language is but poor, yet the statement is authentic.

### BATTLE OF ANTRIM.

On the 7th of June 1798, at 9 o'clock, A. M. an express arrived from General Nugent at Belfast, to Major Siddon of the 22d light dragoons, commanding in the town of Antrim, to inform him, that there was a general rising expected in this county, and that the town of Antrim would be attacked, in order to secure the magistrates who were to meet there by order of Lord Viscount O'Neil, governor of the county.

Major Siddon immediately collected his small forces together, which consisted of one troop of the 22d light dragoons, the Antrim yeomen infantry, (80 in all) commanded by the Earl of Massareene, and about thirty men who voluntarily turned out under the command of one Mr. J. Charters.

This handful of brave men, waited under arms on the parade, (which is at the very lower end of the town) from ten o'clock A. M. until two o'clock P. M. when in an instant the out-posts were driven in, and immediately after about 6000 rebels entered the head of the town, with two brass six-pounders in front, and marched into the church-yard, which is exactly in the middle of the town.

Upon this, the Earl of Massareene made a short but pithy speech to the troops; the yeomen immediately marched up half way to the church, and the light dragoons marched up in the rere. Just as the troops had halted, Lieut. Col. Lumley, with two troops of his regiment, (22d light dragoons) and two curricle guns, came in from Blaris Camp; the yeomen were then ordered to file off to right and left, in order to line the streets, and give room for the cannon to act. Before the horses were unyoked from the guns, the rebels had fired two rounds of cannister shot, which was fifty musket-bullets in a stocking. The salute was soon returned, and the roof of the church being much damaged the rebels fled into the houses and lanes.

Lieut. Col. Lumley imagining this to be a total retreat, ordered the dragoons to charge, but unfortunately the rebels opened so brisk a fire of musquetry from the windows, that the dragoons were

were forced to retreat in great confusion, with the loss of twenty men, one officer, and one quarter-master killed, Lieut. Col. Lumley, Major Siddon, and Lieut. Murphy wounded.

The rebels being greatly elated with this temporary advantage, rushed on furiously in order to surround the yeomenry, who still remained exposed to their fire; upon this the gallant Earl of Massareene was forced to retreat to his own garden, which being surrounded by a lofty wall, was a very proper post. The yeomen had been forced to leave the cannon in the street, but covered them so well by a heavy discharge of musquetry, that the rebels could not touch them, so that they were once more enabled to sally forth, and draw them safely off.

The yeomen continued in this position until four o'clock P. M. during which time they were often furiously attacked by large parties of the rebels, and as often bravely repulsed them. The rebels being worn out by so many vain attempts, retired from the town, and had actually sat down in a field adjacent, and had begun to feast upon large quantities of meat which they had brought with them; when a yeoman who was posted upon the top of Lord Massareene's castle, beheld a large reinforcement upon a neighbouring hill: consisting of detachments of the Monaghan and Fifeshire regiments, under the command of Col. Durham,

Durham, a party of the 22d light dragoons, under the command of Major Smith, and the Belfast cavalry, under the command of Captain Rainey. A yeoman was then immediately dispatched by a private way, bearing a red flag, to inform the army of the situation of affairs; the dragoons immediately pursued, and the foot separated and made great slaughter in the fields.

Upon computation, the rebels lost four hundred men, while the army in killed and wounded, lost about thirty.

The Rt. Hon. Lord Viscount O'Neill, received a mortal pike-wound early in the action, of which he died on the 17th of the same month, at the Earl of Massareene's castle in the town of Antrim.

Nothing could exceed the valour of the troops on this occasion, a remarkable instance of which, was, one Jackson, a young man, and a member of the Antrim yeomen, who having received a mortal wound in his knee, absolutely refused to retreat, until he would discharge his piece at the rebels: this poor young fellow (after suffering an amputation) died, much regretted by every real loyalist in this country.

The rebels were headed in this engagement by M'Givoren, a petty grocer, and an inhabitant of Antrim, and one H. J. M'Cracking, a native of Belfast. M'Cracking was since hanged in the town of Belfast, but M'Givoren has been pardoned.

The

The rebels were so sure of victory, that they brought horses and cars, to carry away the spoil. But the hand of God fought against them, and discomfited all their bloody intentions.

I am Sir,

Your humble Servant,

I. M.

---

LETTER XIV.

FOXFORD, JULY 18, 1799.

*My dear Friend,*

I should have answered yours sooner, but on account of the hurry of military business, as also another reason; which is, that at the time I wrote the letters alluded to,‖ my feelings were more sensible to remark occurrences than at present—but as you have requested the favour, I will transcribe such particulars as I can now recollect.

On Sunday, the third of June, 1798, one hundred and thirty of our regiment (the Armagh militia), commanded by Lieutenant-colonel Cope, marched into Gorey; and in the evening we were joined by different other detachments. We halted there all night, and next morning paraded

‖ *The reader is referred for the accounts of the battles of Arklow and Vinegar-hill, given by this correspondent, to* PART *the* FIRST, *pages* 70, 75.

to the number (yeomenry included) of about eleven hundred brave looking men. I could not suppose that the rebels would have opposed such a force; nor did we expect battle till we arrived at Vinegar-hill; which, I believe, may have been the cause of the insecurity of our commanding-officers, and which led to our defeat. The 4th of June (our gracious King's birth-day—oh! may we never commemorate it with such an awful scene) our forces were divided, one part under the command of General Loftus, the other under that of Colonel Walpole, our fighting general. General Loftus took the main road, leading to Wexford. I was under the direction of the latter, who took a country road, which after a few miles travelling struck out on the former.

### *BATTLE OF TUBBERNERNEEN, near Gorey.*

We marched about three miles, when Colonel Walpole rode along the line on march, and requested of the troops to be in readiness, as he expected an enemy very near; their piquets having appeared within a mile of us. We came to a beautiful situation by nature; the quicksets were very high on either hand, as also a woody country, through which we were to proceed: in this place lay our enemy, to the amount of twelve thousand! They secreted their force behind hedges, to allure us into the ambuscade—which unfortunately

unfortunately answered their hellish design. Our cannon, consisting of two six-pounders, and a small field-piece of the Ancient British fencibles, were ordered to the front—the road became narrow, which prevented the great guns from acting agreeably to our wish: then began a heavy fire of musquetry from each side of the road, and from behind the hedges on our army; which continued on both sides without intermission, for two hours: the cannon ceased, owing to the narrow pass, as also the horses being killed in the traces. We were ordered to take a field in front of their fire: here we disputed the ground for half an hour, when eleven brave fellows of our regiment fell on each side of me. I am now bound in gratitude to acknowledge the kindness of God to me—while loading my piece, the cartridge was taken out of my fingers by a ball, within four inches of my head, and my pantaloons torn across by another—but the issues of life were in the hands of a kind preserver. Col. Walpole received a ball in the thigh, and in a moment after another through the head; by which means this brave soldier fell a victim. A ball went through Colonel Cope's horse's ear, which grazed his cheek, and passed through his hat, while commanding the men—several officers were wounded in like manner. In a little time their line broke, which we took for an omen of

their

their defeat; but this was only to deceive us—for their two wings set up the *war-hoop*, and made for Gorey, to cut off our retreat, which had been ordered to be made. Eighteen of our men, with Colonel Cope and Ensign Collins, were left behind in the meadows—having learned that the body of our army were gone, we were determined to fight our way after them. It was truly painful, as we passed along, to behold our cannon on the roads useless to us—the pikemen with exultation leaping across them, displaying their emblems of disaffection over them, crying " *Erin go bragh*, the English cannon is ours"—also the groans of the wounded, whose bodies, torn and pierced by pikes, while yet living, rendered the scene altogether very awful! we not knowing but this would shortly be our fate: but God was with *us*—we fought, and loaded while running, and endeavouring to avoid the fire of our own cannon, which were turned upon us by the rebels. We passed by Tubbernerneen-rock, where their green flag was displayed, and killed one of their chieftains on horseback; also a number who pressed after us. Arriving at the hill of Gorey (though scarcely able to move), we made another stand, and saved the lives of the Protestants of the town, who otherwise (as they declared) would not have escaped. Numbers who wore *ribbands* as loyalists in the morning, fired out of windows on us at our return—yet not a man fell! In this encounter we loft in killed and miffing, one hundred men, fome of whom we afterwards relieved at Vinegar-hill.

I would here remark the neceffity there is of picquets reconnoitering the country while brigades are on their march, to prevent the enemy from approaching till the troops fhould be prepared to receive them; had this been the cafe, we fhould not have been defeated. After the battle we got to Arklow, where we deftroyed every thing military which we could not take off with us, and returned next day to Wicklow.

P. S. The cavalry made feveral unfuccefsful charges during the battle—they could not act on account of the enclofures. A vaft number of rebels fell on that day, as they fince have acknowledged. Thus have I tranfmitted to you the particulars of this dreadful event, and am, dear friend,

Yours, &c.

W. H. G.

LETTER XV.

KILCULLEN, JULY 20, 1799.

Sir,

The following lines fhall be found as authentic as could poffibly be collected by me, with refpect to the battles of Kilcullen and Old Kilcullen, on the

the twenty-fourth of May, 1798. It will be proper in the first place to premise, that Lieut. Gen. D——s had early information of the rebels intention of rising; and so well was he convinced of it, that he dispatched two men of Captain Latouche's corps of yeomen cavalry, at ten o'clock on the night of the twenty-third (namely Mr. J. Farrange, and Mr. H. Gribbin), to Ballymore-Eustace, to put the troops there on their guard that night. The strength of that town was one troop of the ninth dragoons, commanded by Captain Beevor, and twenty men of the Tyrone militia light company, commanded by Lieutenant M'Farland.

### BATTLE OF BALLYMORE.

The rebels surprised this small garrison about twelve o'clock at night, whilst they were all in bed, except a corporal's guard, consisting of six men, from which a centinel was posted on the residence of the officers, who all lodged in one house. The rebels fired at the centry, whom they left as dead (he is perfectly recovered of his wounds), and then attacked the guard, who fought their way up to the officers lodging, where they met six of the Tyrone, who had assembled with Lieutenant M'Farland—and those men, with a few more, kept up so well-directed a fire, that they routed the rebels, in number not less than one thousand. Many of them were killed. The loss of the army was Lieut. M'Farland, of the Tyrone militia, and four privates, killed—five wounded; the ninth dragoons, six killed and several wounded. The rebels rallied several times, and attempted to come in at different parts of the town, but were always repulsed.

But to return, I have said above, that Mr. Farrange and Mr. Gribbin were sent to Ballymore—they were going on together, conversing, probably not apprehensive of danger, when, behold, they rode in among a body of pikemen that were coming to attack this town! Gribbin happened to be a few yards before Farrange, who instantly wheeled his horse, came back to Kilcullen, and alarmed our little garrison, who were till then perfectly at their ease (Gribbin was severely piked, but is perfectly recovered). In a few minutes our garrison was under arms; it consisted of a Captain (Beale) and twenty of the Suffolk fencibles, Captain La Touche and about thirty of his corps, a serjeant and nine of the Romney fencible cavalry, and a corporal and six of the ninth dragoons. As soon as the alarm was given, all the cavalry went out to scour the country, and the infantry remained patroling from the turnpike to the cross roads, the whole night, till six in the morning. About two o'clock, the cavalry sent in a rebel, who was going to join his

party

party—he was inftantly tied up and flogged—he confeffed that he was going to Mullacafh-hill, to join a large body of rebels, and from thence he faid they were to march to Naas, to attack that place—which they actually did. As foon as he gave this piece of information, an exprefs was inftantly fent to Naas by a dragoon (Mr. H. Barker), to warn them of their danger; but the rebels had reached Naas before the exprefs arrived, and had entered the town at every avenue,‡ and commenced the attack, which lafted but a very fhort time, until they were completely defeated, leaving one hundred and thirty dead in the ftreets and fields, and a vaft number wounded.

The next alarm we had here, was from Judge Downes, who happened to lodge in this town one night, on his way to Cork, I believe to try prifoners on a fpecial commiffion,; he fet off from this about eight in the morning of the 24th, and having got as far as the green of Old Kilcullen, one mile from this town, his poftillion pulled up the horfes, and told his mafter that there were a great number of pike-men at the church, and about the hill—the Judge inftantly drove back, and informed the General thereof, who rode up to meet the rebels, with the Romneys and fuch of the 9th dragoons as were here; in all 15, with Capt. Cooke of the Romneys, and Capt. Erfkine of the 9th.

‡ *See* PART *the* FIRST, *page* 63.     The

## BATTLE OF KILCULLEN.

The rebels were very advantageously posted to act against cavalry, as they occupied the church-yard, surrounded by a parapet wall. As soon as the cavalry had advanced pretty well up the hill, the rebels rushed out of the church-yard, attacked the cavalry with great fury, drove them a considerable way down the green, killed Capt. Cooke, two privates of the Romneys, and two or three horses; they also killed two or three of the 9th, and wounded several of both regiments, then returned exulting to their former position. At this instant arrived Capt. Beale, with 20 men, and about 14 of the loyalists of Kilcullen; the cavalry did not think proper to give the infantry the way, but advanced in great spirits to charge the rebels again, (sword in hand) as they had done before, and were again defeated, with the loss of Capt. Erskine, two or three men and several wounded. The infantry were still pushing forward to the church-yard, where the rebels were again posted after their second charge, and thought they could not be beaten from it; but as soon as the infantry came up, Capt. Beale divided his little party, gave his serjeant the command of six men, and sent him to an opposite part of the wall, to that where the Capt. stood with his men, in order I suppose to obtain a cross-fire on the rebels, who never stood a volley but one, when they fled with great precipitation—there were but five or six of them killed, and some wounded; the rebels wounded one of the Suffolks severely in the hand with a pike, and killed serjeant Clarke of the 9th, who marched up with the infantry, not having a horse to join his own regiment: it was by his own intrepidity he suffered, as he leaped over the wall, and rushed among the throng of the rebels—this terminated the business of that place.

I imagine this business would have been much more serious to the army and loyalists, had it not been for either the policy, or cowardice of *General Perkins*, who was posted on Knockawlin hill, with about 300 pike-men, and when the fight was going on, he and his men advanced running down from the hill to join their comrades, whom they had seen successful against the cavalry, but they halted short, and staid lurking about the ditches, and behind the carman's-inn, when they perceived the infantry had got the better of the rebels at the church. I must here take notice that when the infantry and loyalists were marching forward to attack the rebels at the church, the 14 loyalists were ordered to halt, lest they should be shot through mistake, as they were all in coloured cloaths. Capt. French then came up, and ordered us back to defend the town as well as

we

we could, that we were all surrounded. It was then that we saw Perkins and his men coming down, and we would have been surrounded by them, had it not been for the defeat of their friends at the church. When we came back to Kilcullen, we could discern in the countenances of the men and women, joy mixed with feigned grief: for some hours we found ourselves in a very tickelish situation, every one around us rebels, and did not know the moment they would rise and assasinate us, when we were relieved from our fears, by a party of the Antrim militia, arriving, afterwards a party of the Tyrone militia, and the remainder of the troops from Ballymore who escaped the slaughter. They remained under arms in the street for about an hour and an half, when General Dundas returned from the battle at Old Kilcullen, with the remainder of the troops who went with him, Capt. Erskine's troop of the 9th, from Athy, Capt. Beale's 20 Suffolks and Capt. La Touche's corps of cavalry. At the instant these troops were entering the town, there was word brought in from the turnpike side of the road, that the rebels were very near the town, in great force: they certainly were in force to the amount of 2000, formed into three different columns; the first was the most numerous, and extended across the road, and into the fields on the right and left of it, and were drawn up in good order:

order: they were not more than two minutes march from us, when the intelligence arrived. No time was lost in going out against this great force—the attack commenced on the part of the rebels, by a discharge of fire-arms, not one of which took the least eff ct; their fire was returned by the army most briskly, and after a few vollies the whole rebel line broke, and ran off as fast as their feet could carry them. They were now pursued by both cavalry and infantry, who slew them like philistines—in the course of twenty minutes 460 rebels lay dead; the wounded were very considerable. The army brought in three cart loads of pikes, and a stand of colours, which their valiant Ensign Mr. Pendrose, threw away, thinking them rather cumbersome in his flight: this brave Ensign lived servant with Eyre Powel Esq. Not a single man of the army was hurt in this engagement, except Campbell, the permanent serjeant of Capt. La Touche's yeomen cavalry, who was accidentally shot through the body by one of the soldiers—he is now almost recovered. We thought every thing would be tranquil after this, but in the evening, the whole of the troops and loyal inhabitants, were ordered to evacuate the town, and march to Naas: the inhabitants had not time to bring their effects with them, and the next morning the 25th, the rebels entered the town in great force: men, women and children,

pillaged

pillaged and carried away all the valuables they could lay hands on, and deftroyed the houfes and furniture of the loyalifts.

On the evening of the twenty-fourth of May, 1798, the army which I mentioned being in Kilcullen, together with the loyalifts, marched for Naas, where they arrived about nine o'clock at night. The army was the firft of courfe who were accommodated, and the poor loyalifts were obliged to remain in the ftreets all that night—a very deplorable profpect! but it turned out better than was expected; for they were culled out by order of the Generals, and a proper houfe appointed for them, where they were ferved out with beef, mutton, bread, &c. from the army ftores. Nor had they any other way of getting provifions, for there was not an atom of any kind to be purchafed—all forts of provifion were in requifition for the army. Every day foraging parties were fent out, who brought in great quantities of fat cattle and fheep—bakers and butchers were fet to work;—fo that there was plenty of every kind of provifion that could poffibly be expected in a garrifon that might be faid to be befieged. Notwithftanding all this plenty, our minds were very miferable for a few days, from the conftant alarms both day and night; not an hour paffed with any degree of tranquillity—a vidette would come galloping in, with tidings that

that the rebels were coming in great force; that they would be in in lefs than ten minutes—the drums beating to arms, trumpets founding to horfe, foldiers running to their pofts, both horfe and foot—fome to guard a pafs, others to cover a retreat, others to make a charge, with an army of referve, &c. &c. This was our fituation during the five days I was there; but after the firft day and night, thofe terrors became fo habitual to us, that we did not mind them, but were prepared to meet with undaunted courage any number of rebels; and often have we wifhed they would attack the town either by day or night. And although Naas is a town with very many entrances to it (indeed every back-door furnifhes an entrance), yet every part was fo well guarded, that it was impoffible for any force, without the affiftance of cannon, to attempt coming near it; for at the fouth end of the town is a large hill, immediately contiguous to the road leading into the town, and half the circumference of this hill is furrounded by a wall ten feet high; on this hill were encamped about a company of infantry, with three pieces of heavy cannon, and engineers to work them. At the North end of the town is a very high and large moat, which commands all that quarter where they could poffibly make any attempt; on this moat were two pieces of cannon, with fuitable equipage, and fome some infantry. In fact, every part was so well guarded, that the CROPPIES never made an attempt after the night of the twenty-fourth,‡ for which they suffered woefully, having left sixty-five dead behind them in the streets. Scarcely a day passed but there were several rebels hanged, who were found lurking about the fields; one in particular, Mr. Pat. Walsh of Ballytore, was taken in a field near Naas, hiding in the gripe of a ditch; he was remarkably well dressed, had a bottle of port, bread and cheese, in his pockets when taken. He was brought in, tried, found guilty, and hanged from a sign-post, and afterwards consumed to ashes—a just punishment for what he was guilty of but a few nights before, namely, the burning of a most active fine fellow, Captain Swaine, of the City Cork Royal militia, at Prosperous—see *Part the First*, page 92. This notorious traitor, Walsh, behaved with unparalleled cruelty, to a number of loyal persons; but, blessed be God, his career was short, for only four days had he fought under the banners of an assassinating banditti, till the strong hand of the Lord avenged the cause of innocent blood. Perkins is at present under sentence of transportation, and is in New-Geneva, and as I mentioned before, was general of the rebels at Knockcalling-hill, about

‡ See PART *the* FIRST, *page* 63.

a quarter

a quarter of a mile from the church of Old Kilcullen.

On the twenty-eighth, Thomas Kelly, Esq; of Madden's-Town, near the Curragh, came into Naas, with proposals from Perkins to General Dundas and General Wilford (he is a magistrate, and went to the rebel camp, where by his persuasions he effected terms of peace), which are as follow: " That Perkins would oblige his men (who were now collected to the number of above two thousand) to give up their arms, on condition that his brother should be liberated from Naas gaol (for we brought him a prisoner from Kilcullen), and that General Dundas should approach the camp with only his aid-du-camp's and a file of men." Mr. Kelly having communicated these terms to General Dundas, he instantly dispatched his aid-du-camp, Captain Reeves, to Dublin, to lay the business before Government; nor did General Dundas give Mr. Kelly an answer, until Captain Reeves arrived early on the following morning. I believe the answer he brought to General Dundas was, " to act as he thought most prudent." A short time after Mr. Kelly returned with Perkins, from the rebel camp, and every thing was accommodated as General Dundas thought proper. Perkins returned to the camp, and his brother was liberated, and went under a strong escort of the 9th dragoons, to protect him from the soldiers, who I believe would have preferred a combat with the rebels, rather than compromise the business.

However the day after Perkins and his brother left Naas, General Dundas with part of the army, both cavalry and infantry, with some pieces of artillery, went to Knockealling camp—the troops were placed in a way to surround them, at least to cut them off, when they were once dislodged from the summit of the hill, (which is an amazing strong Danish-fort, surrounded by a very large and deep trench, with a wall within-side) it would not have been easy to dislodge them but by bombs, for which purpose mortars were brought. As soon as the army had made the necessary dispositions, General Dundas with his aid-du-camps, and a few men went forward from the lines, and Perkins with a few of his men approached them and surrendered: the rebels on the hill perceiving this, set off in all directions, huzzaing, I fancy with joy that they were permitted to go to their homes; most in this neighbourhood immediately returned home—a great number from other parts instantly set off for Vinegar-hill. There were no provisions found in the camp, every thing being taken off the day preceding; there were thirteen cart loads of pikes left on it, which were brought into Kilcullen and destroyed. For three weeks they were flocking in from all parts of this district,

taking

taking the oath of allegiance, and getting protections; several notwithstanding were taken shortly afterwards in acts of open rebellion, with these very protections in their pockets, a plain proof of part of their creed " that no faith is to be kept " with a protestant King, or with protestants" whom they call heretics. The next day after the forementioned, a large body of rebels collected on the Curragh, at an old Danish-fort commonly known by the name of *Gibbit Rath*, for the purpose of attacking the City of Dublin militia, who they knew were on their march to Naas, and were to come directly by where the rebels were assembled: now some say that they were collected for the purpose of surrendering; be that as it may, they were the first who violated the treaty, by firing on the troops. You may be sure it was then returned quick enough—they stood but one discharge from the army, when they fled in every direction: Lord Jocelyn's fox-hunters coming up in the instant pursued them and killed 350; there were also wounded a vast number;—the rebels could not have taken worse ground for to make a defence, as there was neither bog nor ditch, to impede their pursuers—those fox-hunters as they are called, certainly would not have left one of them alive, had it not been for the trumpets and bugles having sounded a retreat, in consequence of an express sent by General Dundas from Kilcullen,

cullen for the purpose of preventing the army (which he knew was coming in that direction) from attacking any rebels they should meet: but the express was too late; had it been a few minutes sooner, in all probability much human blood would have been saved. One circumstance happened here, which I cannot pass by unnoticed—the Rev. Mr. Williamson of Kildare, had been brought out by the rebels, who, when the army was approaching, made his escape to them: the Dublin militia insisted he was a priest, heading the rebels, and were so incensed against him, that they were really in the act of fixing a chain belonging to the cannon about his neck, in order to hang him, when his brother-inlaw, Col. Sankey, coming up, convinced them of their mistake, and saved him.—here is one instance of the consequences of civil war, where the innocent often suffer for the guilty: this amiable gentleman narrowly escaped an untimely death, by the precipitancy of those Gentlemen who did not know him.

I have only to add, that on evacuating Kilcullen, the rebels entered, accompanied by an immense croud of women—that while in possession of the same, every species of excess, was resorted to by them—their first object was to plunder the loyal inhabitants houses, drain the cellars and destroy their furniture, &c.—This we have been.
credibly

credibly informed by a loyal woman who had been made prisoner, and whose husband they brought to their camp and shot.—Mr. Flanagan the executioner, ordering him to drop down on his knees, and open his mouth, he thrust a pistol into it, crying aloud as he pulled the trigger, " come you scoundrel, here's a health to King George, " and long may he reign."—Thus fell that loyal old veteran quarter-master King of the 9th dragoons, leaving two sons in same regiment, one of whom was desperately wounded at Ballymore—hoping the foregoing, may answer your intended Work.

I remain, Sir,

Yours, &c.

L. M.

## LETTER XVI.

MONASTEREVAN, AUGUST 1st, 1799.

*Sir,*

With reluctance I recal to mind the deplorable transactions of May 1798. I wish to God they could be buried in utter oblivion; but as that is impossible, and that they will be recorded, a true and faithful narrative should be published.

Our country, previous to the burst of open rebellion, was dreadfully disturbed; frequent murders

ders and affaffinations of loyalifts in open daylight—in fhort, terror was the order of the day; which certainly had the defired effect, of forcing many from their allegiance into the *vortex* of rebellion.

On the twenty-fourth of May, 1798, we had an account that, of two of our lads (I mean of the Monafterevan corps of yeomen), who were in the country on bufinefs, one was barbaroufly murdered, and the other a prifoner; the troop inftantly marched, and made a circuit of feveral miles, to give the loyalifts an opportunity of retreating into Monafterevan, which had the defired effect. They met numbers of thofe deluded people, and had fome partial engagements, in one of which they had the good fortune to refcue three foldiers of the Ancient Britons, part of a detachment marching from Kildare, confifting of a warrant-officer (whom they took prifoner and we refcued next day) and four privates, one of whom they barbaroufly murdered. One of our troop who purfued too far into a bog on foot, was piked in a dreadful manner. The troop then called on Mr. Darrah (feven miles from Monafterevan, who had been defperately wounded fome time before by thefe affaffins, and now drags on a miferable exiftence, deprived of the ufe of his limbs, and in conftant anguifh), in order to bring him and his family in with him; but it was
impoffible

impossible to remove him—his house had been attacked that morning by two or three hundred men, whom they beat off, killing several of them. At this time the country seemed alive with parties of pikemen running in all directions for Kildare, the *focus* of rebellion. The troop then returned home, where they arrived at eight o'clock, and found two companies of infantry who were quartered here, marching off to join General Dundas at Naas, leaving the town entirely to the protection of the yeomen, consisting of forty-three cavalry and forty-two infantry, not three weeks embodied.

### BATTLE OF MONASTEREVAN.

Captain Haystead planted videts, sentries, &c. &c. and the whole stood to their arms at night, every moment expecting an attack; at four o'clock he ordered the men to refresh, but not unsaddle their horses. In a few minutes a videt galloped in, with intelligence that they were coming in great force down the canal. The infantry, under the immediate command of Lieut. George Bagot, formed on the bank of the canal, and the cavalry in the street that runs at right angles with it. When the rebels came within musquet shot, the infantry wheeled and presented —the rebels halted—the infantry recovered arms and advanced; which intimidated them so much, that

that the moment we opened fire they broke. Captain Hayftead then lead the cavalry through a road backwards, to prevent them from getting into the Old Town, which he fuppofed might be their intention: on this road he fell in with a fecond column, and cut through them, killing feveral, and difperfing them completely. He then intended to move through the lower town, to his original fituation, to fupport the infantry, if attacked from the Queen's-county, numbers appearing from that quarter; but when he turned the market-houfe, he perceived the church-yard, which is a commanding fituation, filled with their mufquet-men, and the ftreet with their pikemen —he inftantly called up Lieutenant John Bagot, and they rode forward, to fee if it were poffible to force through them, when Mr. *Garry* of Kildare, who was a principal commander, advanced, and fired a blunderbufs at them without effect— finding they were fo ftrongly pofted, they deemed it madnefs to charge—at this time they had fet part of the town on fire. Captain Hayfted led the troop a wider circuit, through another road, to their original pofition, fighting the whole way, and fortunately called in part of the infantry, who had purfued with confiderable effect thofe who were broke. The fight then commenced defperately in the main ftreet, and continued until twenty minutes paft fix, when the rebels ran in

al

all directions, leaving numbers dead. We had two of our cavalry killed and one wounded, five of our infantry killed, and two of our loyal townsmen (all of whom did their duty most spiritedly) wounded—we had also ten horses killed, and three wounded. From the testimony of several of the rebels, their force exceeded three thousand!

The state of the country, constant fatigue, and our garrison so weak in *number*, prevented us from interring the rebel dead until Saturday at three o'clock, when sixty-eight were put under the clay—numbers, we know, were carried off by their friends. Our men were obliged to stand to their arms, night and day, until the Tuesday following, when Sir James Duff marched in from Limerick.

We have just reason to say, " that though our enemies were many who rose up against us, yet their machinations were vain; for the Lord was our shield and buckler, and mighty deliverer."

You will be so good to inform me when I can get your publication.

    I am, Sir,
     Your obedient servant,
        W. B.

LETTER

## LETTER XVII.

Newtown-Barry, August 12th, 1799.

Sir,

Nothing but your repeated applications, together with the respect I entertain for you, could have induced me to attempt stating the account for which you have so entreated—Capt. K. to whom you say you have written, could certainly do the subject more justice, and your publication service: however, you and the world may rely upon the following to be FACTS.

Sometime previous to the attack upon this village, we were kept in a state of alarm, in consequence of the multiplied reports respecting the rebels—the result was, that our (yeomenry) duty became both constant and severe. On the 1st of June 1798, about twelve o'clock at noon, the rebels (10,000 in number) marched from Vinegar and Lacken hills against our town, fully bent upon exterminating all who should be found inical to their system—they were descried by a reconnoitering party, headed by our gallant Capt. Kerr, as they advanced on both sides of the river Slaney, led on by Doyle, priests Kearns and Redmond, &c.

*BATTLE*

## BATTLE OF NEWTOWN-BARRY.

No sooner had their approach been announced, than our forces prepared to receive them. We had at this time about four hundred of the King's county militia, with two pieces of cannon; eighty of the 4th dragoons, also twenty Carlow cavalry; eighty infantry, and thirty loyalists, to oppose so great an host! "But that the battle is not to the strong," the event fully demonstrated.

The rebels, from an adjacent hill, commenced a brisk fire upon the town from a brass six-pounder, a howitzer, and some ship swivels, accompanied by irregular vollies of musquetry; but without any effect—our position was very strong—every breast burned with ardour for an onset. This was however over-ruled for some time; and by order of Colonel L'Estrange, of the King's-county militia, we retreated a small distance from the town. The rebels concluding we were dismayed, poured into it like a mighty torrent, from the slate quarry, and other hills. You may easily judge the effect such a scene must have had upon those among us, who had both our families, friends, and considerable property therein—all likely to suffer from the ferocity of the ruthless horde—our fears were soon confirmed, as the rebels instantly set fire to the suburbs, plundered the army-baggage, and were proceeding to pillage

many

many houses, when they were most gallantly resisted by a few loyalists from different houses. A universal cry for an immediate attack now ran throughout all the ranks, and after much intreaty was complied with by C. L. It commenced by a few discharges from our cannon—this had the desired effect; it threw them into great confusion, which was increased from the fierce attack we made on them, and the fire from our small arms. Captain Kerr now headed a set of brave fellows, accompanied by Major Marlay, who volunteered on this occasion. We charged the rebels up the hills, pursuing them several miles, all the way cutting them down in great numbers. In their flight they left behind them their cannon-shot, pikes, and some plunder, &c. Upwards of three hundred and fifty were killed—the first complete defeat they had experienced in the county of Wexford. Providentially, our loss was only one loyalist killed, and one of Captain Cornwall's troop wounded.

The rebels, on entering the town, forced into several cellars, &c. where they indulged themselves with such wines and spirits, &c. as came first to hand—nor did they at all suppose they should be dispossessed. They set the church on fire, and had it not been for our success in routing them, many innocent lives would have been forfeited.

This

This victory (which by some may be deemed as inconsiderable) was surely important, on the following account: *First*, it stopped their progress in their intended direction; for had they taken Newtown-Barry, it would have formed an open for them into the counties of Carlow, Kildare, King and Queen's-counties. *Secondly*, it must have clearly demonstrated to them, what a few men will perform when espousing a GOOD CAUSE; and this also should convince them, that the God of armies enabled us to fight this battle. *Thirdly*, Newtown-Barry would have proved a grand *central position*—here they could have collected powerful forces from the collieries and the adjacent counties—all ripe for rebellion. This, no doubt, induced them to attack us, previous to Ross or Arklow; for as I have been well informed, the *rebel plan* was, immediately after their taking Newtown-Barry, to proceed to Arklow, and thence to—Dublin!

The valour of both officers and men was signally great—particularly Lieut. Col. Westenra, Major Marlay, Captain Kerr, of Newtown-Barry troop, and Captain Jennings, 4th dragoons.

Having transmitted to you, Sir, nothing but stubborn facts, I subscribe myself,

Your real friend and well-wisher,

R. W.

IT being the Publisher's particular wish, that this work should prove perfectly correct—he has, for this purpose, left no means untried to accomplish so desirable an end.

In the present PART of this NARRATIVE, it was intended to *detail* the particulars of each subsequent Battle; but for want of Correspondents, in a few places (only), the accounts are stated as they appeared officially.—The honorable situations in which those Gentlemen were placed who wrote them, supersedes the necessity of attempting any thing recommendatory.

It only remains, that should Gentlemen transmit to the Publisher more circumstantial information (not anonymous), such shall be printed as a Supplement to the Work.

*Copy*

*Copy of a Letter from Sir Hugh O'Reilly, Lieut. Col. of the Westmeath Regiment of Militia, to Lieutenant-General Sir James Stewart, at Cork.*

BANDON, JUNE 20, 1798.

Sir,

I have the honor to inform you, that a party of the Westmeath regiment, consisting of two hundred and twenty men, rank and file, with two six-pounders (under my command), were attacked on our march from Cloghnakilty to Bandon, near a village called Ballynascarty, by the rebels, who took up the best position on the whole march.

The attack was made from a height on the left of our column of march, with very great rapidity, and without the least previous notice, by between three and four hundred men, as nearly as I can judge, armed mostly with pikes, and very few fire arms. We had hardly time to form, but very soon repulsed them with considerable loss, when they retreated precipitately, but not in great confusion; and when they regained the height, I could perceive they were joined by a very confiderable force. I, with the greatest difficulty and risk to the officers, restrained the men, halted and formed the greater part of them, when I saw that the enemy were filing off a high flank, with an intent to take poſſeſſion of our guns.

A detachment of one hundred men of the Caithneſs legion, under the command of Major Innes, was on its march to replace us at Cloghnakilty, and hearing our fire, preſſed forward, and very critically fired upon them whilſt we were forming, and made them fly in every direction with great precipitation. At the ſame moment, a very conſiderable force ſhewed itſelf on the heights in our rere. A vaſt number of pikes appeared—ſome with hats upon them, and other ſignals, I ſuppoſe in order to collect their forces. I ordered the guns to prepare for action, and very fortunately brought them to bear upon the enemy with good effect; as they diſperſed in a ſhort time, and muſt have left a conſiderable number dead. Some were killed in attempting to carry away the dead bodies. It is impoſſible to aſcertain the loſs of the enemy, but a dragoon, who came this morning from Cloghnakilty to Bandon, reports that their loſs is one hundred and thirty.

I feel moſt highly gratified by the conduct and ſpirit of the officers and men of the Weſtmeath regiment; and had only to complain of the too great ardour of the latter, which it was almoſt impoſſible to reſtrain. I cannot give too much praiſe to Major Innes, Captain Innes, and all the officers,

officers, non-commiſſioned officers, and privates, of the Caithneſs legion, for their cool, ſteady conduct, and the very effectual ſupport I received from them. Our loſs was one ſerjeant and one private.

I have the honor to be, &c.

(Signed)          HU. O'REILLY,
*Lieut. Col. Weſtmeath regiment.*

---

*Extract of a Letter from Lieutenant-General Lake to Lord Caſtlereagh.*

WEXFORD, JUNE 23, 1798.

My Lord,

Yeſterday afternoon I had the honor to diſpatch a letter to your Lordſhip, from Enniſcorthy, with the tranſactions of that day, for his Excellency the Lord Lieutenant's information;— and the incloſed copy of a letter† from Brigadier-General Moore to Major-General Johnſon, will account for my having entered this place without oppoſition. General Moore, with his uſual enterpriſe and activity, puſhed on to this town, and entered it ſo opportunely, as to prevent it from being laid in aſhes, and the maſſacre of the remaining priſoners, which the rebels declared their

† *See page* 154.                intention

intention of carrying into execution the very next day; and there can be little doubt would have taken place; for the day before they murdered above seventy‡ prisoners, and threw their bodies over the bridge.

Inclosed is a copy of my answer to the proposals of the inhabitants of this town, transmitted in my letter of yesterday to your Lordship: the evacuation of the town by the rebels renders it unnecessary. I have the pleasure to acquaint your Lordship, that the subscriber of the insolent proposals, Mr. Keughe! and one of their principal leaders, Mr. Roache! with a few others, are in my hands without negotiation.

## TERMS PROPOSED BY THE REBELS IN THE TOWN OF WEXFORD.

"That Captain M‘Manus shall proceed from Wexford towards Oulart, accompanied by Mr. E. Hay, appointed by the inhabitants, of all religious persuasions, to inform the officer commanding the King's troops, that they are ready to deliver up the town of Wexford without opposition, lay down their arms, and return to their

‡ *Recent accounts state the number to be ninety-five.*

allegiance,

allegiance, provided that their perfons and properties are guaranteed by the commanding-officer; and that they will ufe every influence in their power to induce the people of the country at large to return to their allegiance alfo. Thefe terms, we hope, Captain M'Manus will be able to procure.

Signed, by order of the inhabitants of Wexford,

MATT. KEUGHE."

## LIEUTENANT-GEN. LAKE'S ANSWER TO MR. KEUGHE'S PROPOSAL.

"Lieutenant-General Lake cannot attend to any terms offered by rebels in arms againft their Sovereign; while they continue fo, he muft ufe the force entrufted to him, with the utmoft energy, for their deftruction.

To the deluded multitude he promifes pardon, on their delivering into his hands their leaders, furrendering their arms, and returning with fincerity to their allegiance.

(Signed)             G. LAKE."

Ennifcorthy, *June* 22, 1798.

*Extract*

*Extract of a Letter from Brigadier-General Moore to Major-General Johnston.*

CAMP ABOVE WEXFORD, JUNE 22, 1798.
*Dear General,*

Agreeable to your order, I took post on the evening of the 19th, near Fooke's-mill, in the park of Mr. Sutton. Next day I sent a strong detachment, under Lieutenant Col. Wilkinson, to patrole towards Tintern and Clonmines, with a view to scour the country, and communicate with the troops you had directed to join me from Duncannon. The Lieutenant-Colonel found the country deserted, and got no tidings of the troops. I waited for them until three o'clock in the afternoon, when, despairing of their arrival, I began my march to Taghmon. We had not marched above half a mile, when a considerable body of rebels was perceived marching towards us. I sent my advanced guard, consisting of the two rifle companies of the 60th, to skirmish with them, whilst a howitzer and a six-pounder were advanced to a cross-road above Goff's-bridge, and some light infantry formed on each side of them, under Lieutenant-Colonel Wilkinson. The rebels attempted to attack these, but were instantly repulsed, and driven beyond the bridge. A large
body

body were perceived at the same time moving towards my left. Major Aylmer, and afterwards Major Daniel, with five companies of light infantry, and a six-pounder, were detached against them. The 60th regiment, finding no further oppofition in front, had, of themfelves, inclined to their left, to engage the body which was attempting to turn us. The action here was for a fhort time pretty fharp. The rebels were in great numbers, and armed with both mufquets and pikes. They were, however, forced to give way, and driven (though they repeatedly attempted to form) behind the ditches. They at laft difperfed, flying towards Ennifcorthy and Wexford. Their killed could not be afcertained, as they lay fcattered in the fields, over a confiderable extent; but they feemed to be numerous. The troops behaved with great fpirit. The artillery, and Hompefch's cavalry, were active, and feemed only to regret that the country did not admit of their rendering more effectual fervice. Major Daniel is the only officer whofe wound is bad; it is through the knee, but not dangerous.

 The bufinefs, which began between three and four, was not over till near eight; it was then too late to proceed to Taghmon. I took poft for the night on the ground where the action had commenced. As the rebels gave way, I was
informed

informed of the approach of the 2d and 9th regiments, under Lord Dalhousie. In the morning of the 21ft, we were proceeding to Taghmon, when I was met by an officer of the North-Cork from Wexford, with the inclofed letters ‡ I gave, of courfe, no anfwer to the propofal made by the inhabitants of Wexford, but I thought it my duty immediately to proceed here, and to take poft above the town; by which means I have, perhaps, faved the town itfelf from fire, as well as the lives‖ of many loyal fubjects who were prifoners in the hands of the rebels.—The rebels fled upon my approach, over the bridge of Wexford, and towards the barony of Forth.

I received your penciled note during the action of the 20th; it was impoffible for me then to detach the troops you afked for, but I hear you have fucceeded at Ennifcorthy with thofe you had. Your prefence fpeedily is, upon every account, extremely neceffary.

I have the honor to be, &c.<br>JOHN MOORE.

‡ *For thefe letters fee pages* 151—3.
‖ *The particulars are given in* PART *the* FIRST, *page* 84.

LETTER

## LETTER XVIII.

Kells, August 14, 1799.

Sir,

On receipt of your first letter, it was my determination to state, for your publication, the particulars of the engagement you so much desired, from the journal I kept. They will be found perfectly accurate, and are as follow—

In the month of May 1798, Captain Molloy, of the Upper Kells infantry, held the arduous situation of commanding-officer at Kells, in the county of Meath. On the 24th he received the following letter by express from Navan.

Tholsel of Navan, May 24, 1798, 5 o'clock.

Sir,

*A private soldier of Captain Gorge's yeomenry, came here about an hour since, and gave us the following account—"That an escort conveying baggage to Dublin, were met on the road leading to Dublin and near Dunboyne, by a body of insurgents—that an attack commenced between them, in which the military were worsted, and every man of the escort killed." It is generally apprehended that the insurgents are on their march to this town, having planted the Tree of Liberty at Dunshaughlin; it is therefore requested that you will be pleased to send immediately such a*

P *a detachment*

a detachment as you can spare here, to assist and protect us. We are, Sir, with much respect, your most obedient servants.

JOHN PRESTON, Captain,
PHILIP BARRY, Lieut. of the
Navan cavalry,

F. D. HAMILTON, Portrieve.

To the officer commanding the garrison at Kells.

On receipt of the above, the yeomen-cavalry and infantry immediately marched off to Navan. There being no appearance of disturbance at that time in the neighbourhood, Capt. Molloy thought it prudent immediately to return to Kells, where there was no protection for the inhabitants, and also a *depot* of ammunition in the town, which particularly demanded his attention: the force in Navan was very inconsiderable, consisting only of the Navan troop. A council of war was called, wherein it was determined that the Kells cavalry, with a detachment of the Navan troop, should go forwards toward Dunshaughlin, and reconnoitre the country. On the 25th the following express arrived from Navan at Kells.

NAVAN, MAY 25, 1798.

SIR,

Prepare your yeomenry immediately, as an insurrection has appeared from Dublin to Dunshaughlin, and

and numbers have been murdered. Communicate this to all the other officers.

Yours, &c.

THOMAS BARRY, Lieut.

*Captain Molloy, Kells.*

This evening two of the Kells cavalry came in express, and brought an account of their seeing the rebel army near Dunshaughlin, on the Dublin side, in great force. Captain Molloy ordered the men who came express to return to their corps, and keep up the communication with Kells, and at the same time sent express to Captain Tatto, of the Bally-james-duff yeomen-infantry, who arrived in Kells at two o'clock, the morning of the 26th, with his corps.

Precisely at three o'clock the same morning, the Upper Kells infantry marched off their parade, resolved to conquer or die—they passed early over Tara. Near Killeen they overtook a party of the Reay fencibles, on their route to Dublin, commanded by Captain Scobie, and also the Upper Kells cavalry, commanded by Lieut. Rothwell, with other corps of yeomen-cavalry—this body arrived at Dunshaughlin about eight o'clock in the forenoon. The country seemed alive with rebels—individuals running from one point to another, but so cautiously and at such a distance,

distance, that they could not be intercepted—at that time it was not known where the main body of the rebels were. Two days preceding this, they entered the town of Dunshaughlin in great force; and in the house of the Rev. Mr. Nelson, murdered him, his brother-in-law Mr. Pentland, and a gardiner, who was a protestant. They also made a prisoner of Mr. Kellett, of the King's-arms; Mr. Ambrose Sharman, attorney, with others; one of whom they also murdered (Mr. Fletcher)—the remainder escaped.

The yeomen's spirits were this day differently affected—at one time elated, hoping to be led on to action—at another depressed; as Capt. Scobie determined not to look for the rebels, but should he meet them on his route would attack them, but not otherwise—his orders were to proceed directly for Dublin. For which purpose he did actually move out of Dunshaughlin, and Captain Molloy resolving not to remain in an enemy's country with so small a body as his corps, determined to return to Kells that day; and had returned out of Dunshaughlin a quarter of a mile for that purpose, but being followed by a friend, was advised not to proceed, as there was a report that the rebels were then encamped on *Tara-hill* in great force, which induced Captain Molloy to form the resolution of overtaking the Reay fencibles, and accompanying them to Dublin; but

as

as the yeomen had advanced to the upper end of Dunſhaughlin, they had the happineſs to ſee the Reay fencibles returning, with whom they marched, and took the field without the town, where the whole regiment remained on their arms till three o'clock that evening; when an officer, who proved to be Captain Blanch of the above regiment, on his return from Dublin, entered the field, with orders it was ſaid to fight the rebels where they could be come up with: On his appearance the men gave three cheers, and were highly animated: they were ordered refreſhment, of which the yeomen equally partook. Three companies of the Reay regiment only, and Captain Molloy's yeomen corps, not amounting to more than one hundred and ninety infantry, with one piece of artillery, were ordered on this expedition, with ſix troops of yeomen-cavalry: theſe troops were placed equally on the right and left of the infantry, in which order they marched from Dunſhaughlin to *Tara*, about five miles.

Before they arrived at Mr. Lynch's houſe of *Tara*, they perceived the rebel videts, both horſe and foot, who immediately wheeled off to their main body, when they perceived the army advancing. On arriving at the large fort at Mr. Lynch's, the army got in full view of the rebel camp on the hill of *Tara;* the fields around appeared

peared black with rebels. On perceiving the army, they inftantly got into motion—their chiefs mounted, and in about ten minutes formed their line, which was extended very far, and very deep, with three pair of green colours.

The rebels availed themfelves of a moft excellent pofition,—the church-yard of *Tara*, furrounded by a wall, which commanded the Dublin road. At this period, that fpirited officer, Capt. Blanch, called the yeomen infantry officers to him, and informed them he had no orders to give, except to lead on their divifions with courage to the action.

### *BATTLE OF TARA.*

And now, commenced an engagement, as eventful for the county of Meath as ever took place therein, and perhaps for the kingdom at large; for had the rebels fucceeded, their numbers would, from partial advantages, have increafed, and in the end, very many would have fallen victims to thofe fanguinary tribes.— But the divine difpofer of all human events conducted our army to, and fecured us victory in this battle. It is our part to return him our continued thanks for the fate of that day.

The

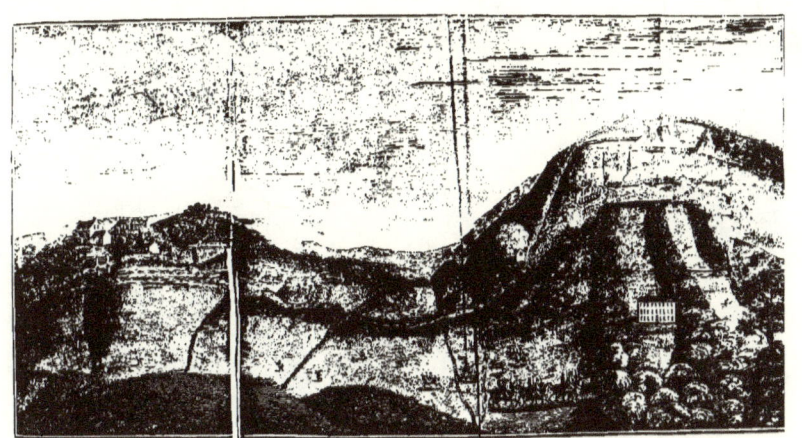

The rebels, upon the approach of the infantry, put their hats † on their pikes, the entire length of their line, and gave three cheers. A person now advanced from their line towards the army (who seemed to assume the command), made a very pompous salute, and returned back with great precipitation—he was dressed in white, was a deserter from the Kildare militia, but imposed himself on many of the rebels for a *Frenchman*, which gave the deluded wretches great spirits.

It was half past six o'clock when the action commenced— immediately some of the army lay dead, from the fire of the rebels. The sixpounder was on the right, from which there were many discharges, but impeded by obstacles between the road and church-yard ;—to obtain the church-yard was the grand object—the little LOYAL PARTY advanced, regardless of danger, notwithstanding the frantic impetuosity and num-

---

† *From concurring accounts it appears, that the* rebel plan *was uniformly adhered to—viz. to annoy the* royal troops *by driving among them such cattle, &c. as they could collect—by endeavouring to dismay them by means of their shouts, and their hats placed on their pikes;—also, when engaged, by exertions to seize the cannon—but what stratagem, what force could have succeeded in such a* cause *?*

ber of rebels who attempted to turn them on each flank, and inceſſantly came down in ſtrong parties, from the church-yard, to the muzzles of their pieces, pike in hand; but they inſtantly experienced the reſult of their temerity, with the loſs of their lives—not one of the royaliſts flinched, though his brother in arms and deareſt friend fell by his ſide. The conflict continued from the period above mentioned (half paſt ſix), until dark, when they gallantly entered the church-yard! The rebels now fled from their ſtrong poſt, and were purſued with great ſlaughter. At this time the cannon was unemployed at the church-yard gate, when a large column of the rebels appeared on the road, with intent to ſurround and cut off a ſmall party of the yeomen who had taken poſſeſſion of the church-yard: Captain Molloy commanded three artillery-men, who remained with the gun, to take it to the road; but he was informed their gunner was killed—upon his aſſiſting they immediately obeyed. The gun was no ſooner placed, than the rebels were at the muzzle; a number actually had their hands on it—the gun being fired made very great carnage. The unexpected diſcharge gave them a very great check—they ſtill perſiſted to ſeize it; for which purpoſe they collected from all points, and made a lodgement behind a wall adjoining the road, which turned to Mr. Brabazon's, zon's, from whence they commenced a heavy fire, but providentially without effect.

Captain Molloy had now ordered that the cannon should not fire till he gave the word.—This encouraged the rebels to advance (supposing the ammunition was exhausted)—they were permitted to come forward in prodigious force, greatly elated; but Captain Molloy here evinced both the wisdom, coolness, and valour of an experienced general, and patiently waited till he had the enemy in such a situation as to do great execution; when he ordered the cannon to fire. This being a few times repeated, determined the fate of the day. In a few minutes not a rebel was to be seen.—Their loss was very considerable. Twenty-six of the Reay fencibles were killed and wounded—one of the Upper Kells infantry killed, and five wounded.

The cavalry had not an opportunity of acting this day (except individually), the country being so close, and the rebels so strongly posted: Lord Fingall behaved with great spirit, and acted as bravely as circumstances would admit, having led on the Navan troop; as also Captain Barnes, who commanded the Lower Kells troop, &c.

The army retired to Dunshaughlin without further interruption, amidst the joyful acclamations of the loyal inhabitants.

Next

Next morning there were some troops sent out to reconnoitre the field of battle, who on their return reported there lay dead on the field, three hundred and fifty of the rebels; many car loads of arms were found, of different descriptions, viz. pikes, musquets, fowling-pieces, pistols, swords, scythes, and reaping-hooks on poles, spits, pitchforks, &c. also three boxes of ammunition, taken from a party of the Reay regiment two days before at Clonee bridge; of whom they killed seven, and took the remainder prisoners (twenty in number), and all the baggage they were escorting to Dublin—the prisoners were retaken at Tara.

Upon the return of the yeomenry to Kells, they were met by a multitude of the loyal inhabitants—welcomed—embraced—the tear of joy sensibly trickled down the cheek of the parent, the sister, the friend—the commanding-officer was presented with a laurel wreath ornamented with ribbons, prepared by the principal people in the neighbourhood—on entering the town of Kells, a groupe of ladies surrounded Captain Molloy, one of whom crowned him with laurel —the windows were decorated with emblems of victory—the bells rang—an elegant collation was laid out opposite the boarding-school, under the shade of some large sycamore-trees—the evening was

was devoted to mirth and joy—age and youth vied in loyal and convivial harmony.

Were I to recount the brave conduct of each yeoman individually, it would no doubt be grateful to the reader; but time and circumstances not permitting, oblige me to decline it. The officers of the Kells corps deserve every compliment this country can give; Lieutenants Keating and Warner, conducted themselves with that spirit and bravery which ever distinguishes the brave soldier—and as for Captain Molloy, the result of that day will ever keep him in the recollection of his friends and acquaintance.

P.S. To the memory of the brave men who fell in the field, the corps are erecting a handsome monument at Kells, with a suitable epitaph.

Thus, Sir, have I particularized every thing I supposed in any wise interesting—and am with great respect,

Yours, &c. &c.

THE affairs of the Northern parts of this Kingdom having been ingeniously epitomised by a very intelligent Gentleman (a resident in Belfast), and transmitted to the Editor—he inserts every sentence of the same; from a conviction, that should any part undergo alterations, the whole would most certainly suffer thereby.

This correspondent, very politely, gives such permission—but surely those who are, or desire in the least to be, acquainted with the rise and progress of the IRISH REBELLION of NINETY-EIGHT, will readily concur with the Editor, that no occurrence tending to pourtray and expose the *concerted measures* of the enemies of the Constitution, should be considered as too minutely described.

## LETTER XIX.

BELFAST, SEPTEMBER 3, 1799.

Sir,

YOU have at length the promised sketch, which it was absolutely out of my power to have done sooner; and which, now that I send it, you will think, perhaps, unnecessarily *minute*.—But, however, you will observe, I leave you the most *absolute* liberty to *prune* away and to *condense* as you think proper—and do *really* wish you on *no account* to retain a single line you may judge superfluous or unnecessary.

When the work is finished, please intimate the same to

Your obedient servant.

## AFFAIRS OF THE NORTH.

LET us now turn our attention towards the NORTH—a part of the kingdom it was supposed there was most peculiar reason to dread; as well from the sturdy character of its inhabitants, as from its early attachment to *French* principles, and being the quarter in which the system of *United Iricism* had originated, which had afterwards spread so very generally over the whole kingdom.

It may not be here improper to obferve, that fo far back as September 1796, feveral perfons were arrefted in Belfaft, as well as other parts of the North; and that it was in March 1797, General Lake, who commanded the Northern diftrict, iffued from Belfaft his proclamation (which made fo much noife), for the bringing in of arms, ammunition, &c.—arrefts occafionally taking place up to the period we are now treating of; a little before which General Nugent had fucceeded General Lake in the command.

The news of the burning the Northern mail coach, was received in Belfaft early on Friday morning, the 25th of May, and of courfe excited very confiderable alarm—but it was not till next morning it was generally underftood the rebellion had actually broke out, and that the burning of the mail-coaches was the *concerted fignal* of infurrection. Numbers of the inhabitants, who had not hitherto been members of any yeomenry corps, made an immediate offer of their fervice to General Nugent; in confequence of which two fupplementary corps, of fixty men each, were formed, and almoft immediately complete—to be clothed at their own expence, and to receive nothing from Government but arms and accoutrements. Indeed, fuch numbers preffed forward to be inrolled, as would have completed feveral companies more, had the General thought

prop:

proper to accept of all who offered on the occasion. However, the four old companies, as well as the troop of cavalry, were strongly augmented; while arms were put into the hands of a number of loyal and well-affected persons, who did duty along with the military—and many of the more wealthy inhabitants, who were prevented by age or infirmity from taking a more active part, subscribed largely towards the better supporting the families of those in the yeomenry, who, when on permanent duty, had little but their pay to depend on.

On Sunday forenoon, martial-law was proclaimed in town by sound of trumpet, and the inhabitants forbidden from appearing in the streets after nine at night, or before six in the morning. In the course of the ensuing week a number of persons were taken up, and either committed to the provost, or sent on board the prison-ship in the harbour; while several who were strongly suspected to be well acquainted with what was going on, were publicly whipped—in order to extort confession. Another proclamation respecting bringing in arms, &c was issued by the General—soon after which a very general search took place in town—almost every house was examined—notwithstanding which, the number of arms procured was very inconsiderable—partly from the numbers already given up, in consequence of the former proclamations, and from many, no doubt, having concealed them, not so much, perhaps, on the principle of disloyalty, as of defending themselves against ruffians of any description.

About this time, two of the four brass field-pieces, formerly belonging to the Belfast Volunteers, were found buried in a back-yard off one of the principal streets—they had eluded every search that had been made about them for above five years, and very probably even then would not have been discovered, but for the threats of the General against the persons in whose custody they were known about that time to have been—when, in consequence of a paper being circulated, very generally signed by the inhabitants, pointing out the impropriety of further concealment at such a crisis, and the consequences that must result to innocent individuals, anonymous information was at length given to the General respecting them, who gave strict orders no injury should be done to the premises on which they were found. Next morning the other two pieces were found lying on the county Down shore, within half a mile of the town, and all brought in by the military, with no small marks of exultation.

Monday, the fourth of June, being the King's birth-day, the regulars, together with the yeomenry

menry-corps, fired three *feu de joie's* in the main-street—in the evening the most general and brilliant illuminations took place ever known there; when, very much to the credit of the General, the troops were all kept in barrack till between nine and ten o'clock, when the entire garrison, horse, foot, artillery with their cannon, and yeomenry, marched through the principal streets. The inhabitants upon this occasion were indulged with liberty of walking about till ten o'clock, when not the slightest irregularity was committed either on the one side or the other.— Indeed, were an opinion to be formed of Belfast from the behaviour of its inhabitants upon that day, at its *feu de joie's*, and during the illuminations, a more loyal town scarcely could have been found in his Majesty's dominions.

Nothing material occurred till Thursday, the seventh of June, when a very general alarm was excited, from the General having received undoubted information that a rising would that day take place in the county of Antrim; the object of which was, among other things, to seize upon the magistrates,‡ who were to meet in the *town* of Antrim, to consider on what measures should be adopted for the peace of the county—the

‡ *For the particulars of the battle of Antrim, see page* 116.

barriers were closed early in the morning, several persons were arrested, and no person suffered to leave the town—though no one was prevented from coming into it. The General had early in the morning directed Colonel Clavering of the Argyleshire, who commanded at Blaris camp, about nine miles from Belfast, to proceed immediately to Antrim, with a detachment of his own regiment and of the 22d dragoons, with two pieces of artillery. About eleven o'clock, detachments from the Monaghan, Fifeshire, 22d dragoons, and Belfast cavalry, with two pieces of cannon, making in all about four hundred men, under the command of Colonel Durham of the Fifeshire, marched also from Belfast to Antrim, where Colonel Clavering's detachment had arrived some time; the cavalry of which had made an unsuccessful attack on the rebels, who had got possession of the town, in which Colonel Lumley was wounded, &c. &c.

After giving the troops some time to refresh themselves, and coolly reconnoitering the position of the rebels, a general attack was made on all points, when they were soon routed; abandoning two curricle guns they had taken on getting possession of the town, as also a brass gun of their own, mounted on a car, which they had fired several times during the action. They were pursued with considerable slaughter, towards Shane's-castle caftle and Randalftown—in which laft mentioned place, a number of houfes were fet fire to, belonging to people implicated in the rebellion.—Some few feeble attempts were afterwards made, on that and the next day, at Larne, Ballycaftle, and Ballimena, but they were foon put down. The rebels in this county appearing immediately afterwards wavering and difpirited; deferting their camps (as their places of affemblage were called), and throwing away or bringing in their arms to the neareft civil or military magiftrates, with the ftrongeft marks of forrow and repentance—the detachment from Belfaft came into town next day, about three o'clock.

Information being by this time received, that a general rifing was on the point of taking place in the county of Down, and that a confiderable number were already affembled near Saintfield, ten miles from Belfaft, General Nugent directed Colonel Stapleton, of the York fencibles, who lay with his regiment at Newtown-Ards, fix miles from Belfaft, and about eight from Saintfield, to march immediately to attack them, before they gathered further ftrength. The Colonel accordingly left Newtown-Ards early next morning, Saturday the 9th, with his regiment, its two battalion guns, and accompanied by the Comber and Newtown-Ards cavalry—the baggage of the regiment having been previoufly fent to Belfaft.

When

When they had proceeded within about a mile of Saintfield, on a most uncommonly hot day, and the country through which they marched, in a great measure deserted, they fell in with a man on the road, very probably thrown in their way on purpose, who informed the commanding-officer, that the rebels were straggling about; were under no sort of order; many of them drunk in the streets; and that they would never dare face the King's troops. This may be presumed to have put them something off their guard—be that as it may, two or three of the yeomen-cavalry did actually go at a gallop to the end of the town; and returned without seeing the appearance of any thing hostile—of course they renewed their march with confidence, not dreaming of the enemy they sought being so near, until they came to a part of the road where there was a number of trees on each side; when, in an instant, the yeomen-cavalry and light company, who formed the advanced guard, were opened upon from behind the ditches by a very heavy fire of musquetry; the pikes at the same time darted across the road—by which, in a very short time, they suffered exceedingly, both in killed and wounded; the main body too was thrown into confusion—but having at length got their cannon into a good position, where they were of the most signal service indeed, they succeeded in

instantly

inſtantly and completely repulſing the rebels; who went off, after ſuſtaining much loſs. Night approaching, the Colonel did not think proper to proceed to Saintfield, which was in the very heart of the country ſuppoſed moſt particularly difaffected—he therefore fell back to Comber, where the troops reſted that night, and came into Belfaſt the forenoon of next day, having ſuffered moſt ſeverely from fatigue and the extreme heat of the weather.

This day, Sunday the 10th, the ſpirit of inſurrection appearing not at all to be checked; but rather gaining ground in the county of Down, numbers of people from the country crowded into Belfaſt, Liſburn, Downpatrick, &c. as to places of greater ſecurity. Belfaſt, at this time, preſented the appearance of a place in a ſtate of ſiege—parties of horſe and foot continually paſſing and repaſſing—the avenues to the town ſtrongly guarded—cannon placed in the principal ſtreets, and three pieces planted on the very long bridge that ſeparates Belfaſt from the county of Down.—In ſhort, every precaution was taken that prudence could ſuggeſt, to give the rebels a warm reception, had they been raſh enough to attack the town; but they never once approached it.

On Monday, the 11th of June, the county Antrim people continuing to bring in their arms,

and

and appearing completely sensible of their folly, the General issued a proclamation, addressed to the county of Down, calling on them to follow the example of their brethren in the county of Antrim, by bringing in their arms, giving up their leaders, and returning to their allegiance—in which case, promising them pardon and protection, giving them twenty-four hours to consider of it. This proclamation was sent through the country by patroles, as generally as the then unhappy state of the country would admit; but such was the infatuation of the people, it was spurned at with contempt; so that it soon became evident the sword only could bring them to reason. Preparations were accordingly made for that purpose; and next morning about ten o'clock, the weather being still most uncommonly warm, the General left Belfast, at the head of the Monaghan and Fifeshire regiments, about one hundred and thirty of the 22d dragoons, with six pieces of cannon and two howitzers, and proceeded to Saintfield, where the rebels were collected in great force—the York fencibles proceeding at the same time to Comber, where they remained, to act as circumstances might require—and here, Sir, I would refer you to the account forwarded by General Nugent to Government of this day's business.‡

‡ *This had been published officially.*

Dublin

*Dublin Castle,* 11 *o'clock,* A.M. *June* 14, 1798.

Intelligence is just arrived from Major-General Nugent, stating, that on the 11th instant, he had marched against a large body of rebels, who were posted at Saintfield. They retired on his approach to a strong position on the Saintfield side of Ballynahinch, and there made a shew of resistance, and endeavoured to turn his left flank; but Lieutenant-colonel Stewart arriving from Down, with a pretty considerable force of infantry, cavalry, and yeomenry, they soon desisted, and retired to a very strong position behind Ballynahinch.

General Nugent attacked them the next morning, at three o'clock, having occupied two hills on the left and right of the town, to prevent the rebels from having any other choice than the mountains in their rear for their retreat; he sent Lieutenant-colonel Stewart to post himself with a part of the Argyle fencibles, and some yeomenry, as well as a detachment of the 22d light dragoons, in a situation from whence he could enfilade the rebel line, whilst Colonel Leslie, with part of the Monaghan militia, some cavalry, and yeomen infantry, should make an attack upon their front. Having two howitzers and six six-pounders with the two detachments, the Major-General

General was enabled to annoy them very much, from different parts of his position.

The rebels attacked, impetuously, Colonel Leslie's detachment, and even jumped into the road from the Earl of Moira's demesne, to endeavour to take one of his guns; but they were repulsed with slaughter. Lieutenant-colonel Stewart's detachment was attacked by them with the same activity, but he repulsed them also, and the fire from his howitzer and six-pounder soon obliged them to fly in all directions. Their force was, on the evening of the 12th, near 5000.

About four hundred rebels were killed in the attack and retreat, and the remainder were dispersed all over the country. Major Gen. Nugent states, that both officers and men deserve praise, for their zeal and alacrity on this, as well as all occasions; but he particularly expresses his obligations to Lieutenant-colonel Stewart, for his advice and assistance throughout the business, and to Colonel Leslie, for his readiness to volunteer the duty at all times. The yeomenry behaved with extreme steadiness and bravery. Three or four green colours were taken, and six one-pounders, not mounted, but which the rebels fired very often, and a considerable quantity of ammunition. Their chief was Munro,* a shopkeeper of Lisburn.

* *He was afterwards hanged.*

Major

Major-General Nugent regrets the loss of Captain Evatt, of the Monaghan militia; Lieut. Ellis of the same regiment was wounded; the loss of rank and file was five killed, and fourteen wounded. Several of the yeomen-infantry were killed or wounded.

———

In the mean time, detachments from the Tay fencibles at Carrickfergus, and the Argyleshire at Blaris, marched in, and in conjunction with the Belfast and Castlereagh yeomenry, with the loyal inhabitants, took charge of the town. Immediately on the troops marching out, orders were issued to shut up every house and shop; centries were placed at the end of every street, and no one upon any account to appear in the streets but those to whom the care of the town was committed—precautions thought necessary to be taken lest any thing improper should be attempted in so critical a moment, in the absence of so considerable a part of the garrison:—every thing, however, continued perfectly tranquil, both in the town and neighbourhood, as well then as during the whole time of the rebellion. In this state, so exceedingly awful and interesting to the inhabitants, anxiously waiting the event, actuated by various, and no doubt, in many cases, by very opposite sensations, the town remained until the forenoon of next day—when news arriving of the

the King's troops being completely victorious, the restrictions were taken off.

General Nugent, with the troops, returned to Belfast, about four in the afternoon of Wednesday, bringing along with them six small iron guns, and several green standards taken from the rebels; and were received in town with the strongest demonstrations of joy. That evening, the Lancashire regiment of dragoons, which had that day landed at Carrickfergus from Scotland, came into town—a day or two after the arrival of the Lancashire, the Sutherland fencibles, 1000 strong, also arrived from Scotland; both arrivals giving no small confidence to the loyal and peaceable inhabitants.

After the affair at Ballynahinch, the rebels were completely dispersed, never afterwards appearing in any part of the North—great numbers were taken up, among whom were many of their leaders; some were transported, others had permission given of going with their families to America, and not a few suffered the punishment of death. While humanity cannot but feel for the many who forfeited their lives on the occasion, it will be acknowledged, at least by the moderate and the impartial, that no inconsiderable portion of lenity was shewn; and that fewer executions took place, every thing considered, than might have been expected—perhaps a smaller number

number than, under similar circumstances, would have been the cafe under any other government in Europe—for, furely, blood has not been the characteriftic of Cornwallis.

It has, no doubt, been matter of fome furprife to many, that the efforts of the North, which had been fo much and fo long fpoken of, fhould have been fo feeble, and of fuch fhort duration— as the rebellion was completely extinguifhed there within a fingle week after it broke out!

The number of perfons who joined the focieties of United Irifhmen in the North, was no doubt very confiderable indeed; but their motives were very different, and their numbers no doubt much exaggerated, for very obvious reafons. It is a fact, however, well afcertained, many became members from policy—from fear—from perfuafion—from motives of private intereft—and not a few of thofe who became fo with cordiality, never conceived the object to be beyond a parliamentary reform—of courfe, from thofe of this defcription, no cordial co-operation could be given.

The precautions then taken by Government, fo far back as the year 1793, in preventing the importation of arms and ammunition—the number of perfons who were difarmed—the early arreft and clofe confinement of fo many of their leaders—and the repeated difappointment in the

expected

expected succours from France, must have altogether tended exceedingly to cool and to embarrass. Besides which, the oppressive and tyrannical conduct of the French; particularly of late, towards those countries who had received them with open arms, and to whom they had promised *liberty* and *peace*, had caused a very considerable change among the sensible and thinking part of the community; who began at length to imagine, they might possibly not act towards Ireland with a greater degree of disinterestedness. Be that as it may, when the rebellion did break out, the people in general were not so hearty in the cause as they would very probably have been some years before. And what, perhaps, contributed more than any other thing to prevent any further attempts, was, the horrid cruelties commited by the Catholics, particularly in the county of Wexford; which induced numbers of the Presbyterians to imagine, were they even to carry their point, the business would be but half done, and that they would have to fight the battle out again with them—a supposition strongly sanctioned by the dying declaration of *Dickey*, a rebel leader, who was executed at Belfast in June, 1798.

May this land never again witness a repetition of such distressful scenes! And may what has already past make a deep impression on the minds of of both *governors* and *governed*—upon the owner of the foil and the useful cultivator of the land—teaching the one to pay every juft attention to the fair and reafonable wifhes of the people, and to meliorate, as much as poffible, the fituation of their tenantry (and much, much indeed of the future tranquillity of the country, depends on a proper attention to this point)—and upon the other hand, teaching the people not to be foolifhly carried away by vifionary and romantic ideas of perfection, that never have, and never can be realized in any government on the face of the earth.

## LETTER XX.

### HACKET's-TOWN, SEPTEMBER 12, 1799.

Sir,

HAVING been requefted to give an account of the tremendous battle of Hacket's-town, on the 25th of June 1798, which has never yet appeared in print, I fend it to you, and you may rely on its authenticity, as I had it from a perfon who was on the fpot, and in whofe words I give it to you.

I am, Sir,
Your humble fervant,
W. B.

ON Sunday, the 17th of June, the rebels, with Garret Byrne of Ballymanus, at their head, were proceeding to attack the town of Hacket's-town,‡ and had resolved to commence their operations early on the 18th; in order to which, they halted about four miles distant, on a hill near the village of Tinahely, called Mount Pleasant, from whence they resolved to proceed next morning at day break. Having several pieces of artillery, the garrison would have been an easy prey to them, had it not been for the interference of Divine Providence. The troops in the neighbourhood had begun to march from their respective quarters, in order, as was supposed, to surround and entirely cut off the rebel forces. In consequence of this motion, General Dundas marched with his brigade into the town, about two o'clock, and had scarcely alighted from his horse, when information was brought that the rebel forces had taken possession of Mount Pleasant, and were destroying Tinahely—he immediately ordered Lord Roden, with his fine regiment, Captains Wainright and Hume, with their yeomen-cavalry, to go and reconnoitre; and se-

‡ *The reader is referred to* PART *the* FIRST, *page 67, for an acccount of the first attack at Hacket's-town.*

veral

veral corps of infantry to cover their retreat, in cafe they fhould be attacked and overpowered by numbers. As foon as the reconnoitering parties came tolerably near them, the rebels fired fome cannon-fhot, on which Lord Roden fent to Gen. Dundas for orders, who defired the parties immediately to retreat into the town. On the retreat of the troops, the rebels fell back to Kilcavan-hill, within two miles of Carnew, where they feemed refolved to await the event of a battle.

On Monday the 18th, General Dundas's brigade was under arms at three o'clock in the morning, and marched at four. General Loftus and his brigade alfo marched from Tullow, and joined General Dundas at Coolattin, about two miles and a half from the hill. The troops had juft got within cannon-fhot, when General Lake and his fuite arrived, and fhortly after, they advanced in column to attack the rebels, who were very advantageoufly pofted on the fummit of a very high hill (Kilcavan), which commanded a great tract of country.

### BATTLE OF KILCAVAN-HILL.

The troops began by firing a few large guns, but without effect, infomuch that when the third gun was difcharged, the rebels gave three cheers, and then began to open a fmart fire on his Majefty's forces; and had not the column which began

began the attack been ordered into line, before the rebels began to fire, there muſt have been many lives loſt—for their firſt ſhot would have raked the column from the front to the rere; and did actually plough up the ground which had not been a minute receded from by the troops. A party then, with a howitzer, got ſomewhat on their flank, and threw in a few ſhells, which did ſome miſchief; and there were a few ſhots of ſmall arms exchanged, but without very great effect.—After which, General Lake thought it prudent to retire to Carnew for the night, during which the rebels evacuated the hill, and retreated to Vinegar-hill—to concentre them at which place, and to cut them totally off, ſeemed to be the deſire and intention of the commanders.

After halting at Carnew the 19th, the troops advanced towards Vinegar-hill;\* the reſult of which is too well known to require repetition — I can only ſay, that the rebels being allowed to eſcape that day from Vinegar-hill, was the cauſe of incalculable miſchiefs to the country;—for after their eſcape they did not conſider that they were *allowed* to get off, in hopes that they would be brought to a ſenſe of their ſituation, and induced to return to their allegiance, but immediately began to undertake new plans of miſchief.

\* See PART *the* FIRST, *page* 74.

And therefore Garrett Byrne collected all his forces at the Seven Churches, on the 22d of June, to attack the town of Hacket's-town; which was a post of great consequence, as it was the key between the counties of Wicklow and Carlow; and being possessed of that, they would have had great advantages, did they but know how to avail themselves of them. Accordingly, on Sunday morning the 24th, the rebel army, amounting to upwards of thirteen thousand men, (of whom there were eleven hundred armed with firelocks, and the remainder with pikes) marched forward to attack the town, and at five o'clock, on Monday the 25th, in the morning, appeared within a mile of it. On the 24th, in the evening, some of the loyalists came into the town, reporting that the rebels were on their march; and there were expresses instantly sent off to beg assistance from all the gentlemen commanding yeomenry corps in the neighbourhood—in consequence of which, Captain and Lieutenant Chamney, with thirty men; Lieutenant Braddell and about thirty cavalry, marched in at half after five o'clock on the 25th;—so that the whole garrison, consisting of fifty Hacket's-town infantry, under the command of Captain Hardy; forty Antrim militia, under Lieutenant Gardiner; thirty Shillelagh cavalry, under Lieutenant Braddell; forty Talbot's-town cavalry, under Captain Hume;

Hume; and thirty Shillelagh infantry, under Captain Chamney, paraded a quarter before six, and marched out to meet the rebels.

## BATTLE OF HACKET'S-TOWN.

When they came within musquet-shot, the garrison began the attack; but such was the numbers of rebels, that they filed off in different directions to surround his Majesty's forces; which obliged the two corps of cavalry to retreat. After the departure of the cavalry, the infantry, amounting in all to one hundred and twenty men, retreated into the barracks, resolved to sell their lives as dearly as possible.

In this retreat, poor Captain Hardy received a ball, which broke his thigh, and some of the yeomen fell; the rebels entered into the town in all directions, set fire to every house but one, by the special orders of Garret Byrne, and threw the gallant but unfortunate HARDY, still alive, into the flames—by which a most valuable life was lost to his country and friends, and a considerable sum of money, which he carried about him, was lost to his family.

The Rev. Mr. Magee, a most decided active magistrate, had with a few loyalists thrown themselves into a house, which stood on an eminence, and completely flanked the barracks;—in this house

house Mr. Fenton, Lieutenant of Mr. Hume's cavalry, was confined by a severe fall he got a few days before in charging the rebels; Mrs. Magee and her children; Mrs. Fenton and her children; and many others, who had fled thither for protection, were assembled—fortunately there was some powder and three musquets in the house, and Mr. Magee and the loyalists made every preparation for a spirited and vigorous defence.

At five in the morning the attack commenced, and the rebels proceeded to the barracks; they met a most warm reception from the troops, and from the fire of two excellent marksmen (who had thrown themselves into the house, through a desire of assisting their neighbour, Mr. Fenton), and who, by taking the rebels in flank, threw them into great disorder; but such was their numbers, fresh forces still poured down, and the battle raged with unceasing fury until two o'clock, the rebels constantly throwing their wounded men into the burning houses, caused a horrid stench. At length the rebels perceived that whilst *this house* was occupied they had no chance of succeeding against the barracks; they, therefore, deserted their attack on the barracks, and solely directed it against what might be well termed FORT MAGEE! The noted *Reynolds*, who had
commanded

commanded at the attack of Naas, lead, on horseback, a desperate party to the rere of the house, whilst another approached the front, under cover of a horse and car with a heap of beds. Immediately Mr. Magee had the roof of the house stripped; and got the marksmen in the upper story, who then overlooked the rebels who were behind the beds, and soon dispatched them; and then turning to the rere, *Reynolds* was brought to the ground by a shot through the belly; on which the assailants of the house, who had survived the attack, fled, leaving the car and beds behind them, and a considerable number of slain. From this period the fire of the assailants began to slacken, but they were repeatedly rallied and brought back to certain discomfiture, until seven o'clock, when they finally retreated, first butchering every loyalist (man, woman and child) they could meet.

The heroic courage displayed by two ladies, the wife ‖ and daughter of Lieutenant Fenton, deserves particular notice—he had struggled out of bed to a chair, where he spent the day making cartridges, whilst his wife and daughter (a beautiful girl) were encouraging, by their conduct, their few but gallant defenders; and when their

‖ *Sister to Captain Rawson of the Athy Loyalists.*

ammunition

ammunition began to fail, these ladies melted down some pewter into balls, and were almost constantly administering meat, wine, and water, to the poor fellows, who were exhausted with fatigue and thirst from the flames of the adjacent houses, and the smoke constantly driving into the windows.—The two principal marksmen in the house were men of a very religious cast, and they never fired a shot without some pious ejaculation, which appeared to be accepted by Providence; as they never pulled a trigger without good effect; frequently, with the pewter bullets, bringing down *four* and *five* at a time! The whole of this wonderful defence was conducted from the house, without a drop of blood being spilled, save a slight wound in the face, which Mrs. Fenton's father (Mr. Rawson) received. The conduct of Lieutenant Gardiner, and the brave men under his command, is above all praise; and they also escaped with a very trifling loss.

When the rebels retreated, the garrison considered it would be imprudent to continue longer in their present situation; it was then determined to march for Tullow (eight miles), but the difficulty was, the removal of Lieutenant Fenton— here the finger of Divine Providence appeared very conspicuous; for, but for the *horse* and *beds*, (no other being to be had), he could not be removed.

Worn down with fatigue, their properties all deftroyed, but with hearts overflowing with gratitude to the Great Difpofer of events, for their wonderful deliverance, the loyalifts, men, women and children, arrived fafe at Tullow, where they experienced every comfort the liberal inhabitants could beftow.

In the houfe with the loyalifts, during the whole of the engagement, were the wives of Garret Byrne and of the rebel General Perry. Brave fouls will always be generous—they were treated with every attention and refpect.

The difcomfited rebels next day burned the barracks and ftores, and laid wafte the houfes of the loyalifts for many miles round.—Lieutenant Fenton's houfe and large property were entirely deftroyed.

Few events, in the courfe of the rebellion, ought to make the loyalifts more confirmed in their adoration of that SUPREME BEING, whofe ftrong arm has, in this extraordinary inftance, fhewed the wicked, that " the battle is not to the ftrong." And it fhould convince the rebellious, that while their works are evil, they will never meet fuccefs. *May the loyalifts endeavour to fecure a continuation of fuch wonderful interventions of Providence in their favour!*

LETTER

## LETTER XXI.

RATHANGAN, SEPT. 12, 1799.

Sir,

AS you have not been so fortunate as to procure the particulars at Rathangan, I send you a brief statement.

The late Mr. Spencer, who commanded the *Rathangan* yeomenry, was unfortunate in appointing a Mr. Molloy lieutenant of his corps, a Roman Catholic and a rebel, who was hanged for the active part he took at Rathangan, and whose influence had the most baneful effect, in seducing from their allegiance the principal part of the cavalry—I mention this, to account for the poor support Mr. Spencer received from his corps.

On Saturday, the 26th of May, his house was attacked by a numerous banditti, headed by Captain Darley (a tenant of his own), and every promise of safety held out if he would surrender; but the instant the doors were opened the villains rushed in, and murdered him and three loyal protestants—the rest of the people, being Roman Catholics, were not injured in the least. They then marched with great exultation to the town of Rathangan, bringing Mrs. Spencer with them, and immediately held out the same false promises to Captain Moore (who had taken refuge with a part of the infantry who were loyal, in his house), and unfortunately succeeded—he judging of them from his own honest good heart. A thousand oaths they swore, that not a hair of their heads should be injured, if they gave up their arms and surrendered; but the moment they opened the door they were seized, and with most violent execrations all murdered in the street;—poor Mrs. Spencer, Mrs. Moore; in short, all the unfortunate females of the town looking on at the dreadful butchery of their husbands, fathers, brothers, and friends. Eighteen were thus massacred, *all Protestants!* not a single Roman Catholic hurt, although there were some of them in the house with Mr. Moore. The rebels remained in undisturbed possession of the town until Monday morning, when a detachment of the 7th dragoons, and some yeomenry from Tullamore, attacked them, but were beat off, with the loss of one officer made prisoner, four privates and two yeomen killed. This gave them such savage confidence, that they were determined to put every Protestant to death; but fortunately for *them*, Colonel Longfield, with a detachment of the City of Cork militia, two curricle guns, and a part of the 5th dragoons, or green horse, arrived, and cleared the town of those miscreants

in

in a few hours after, killing about fifty of them, without the loss of a man, and but two or three wounded. If any thing further occurs to you, necessary for your information, I shall be happy in communicating it to you, if in my power.

I remain, Sir,<br>Your obedient servant,<br>W. B.

---

## LETTER XXII.

ATHY, SEPT. 17, 1799.

Sir,

THE first part of your Narrative of the Irish rebellion informs me, we are soon to be favoured with a continuation of those melancholy, yet highly interesting events, which occurred in the year 1798. Should you not have received the particulars of the attack at *Providence*, Queen's-county, I make bold to transmit you a summary thereof; fully assured (though it should appear to some uninteresting) it will be gratefully received in that part of the kingdom.

On the morning of the twenty-fourth of May, 1798, a party of rebels, fifteen hundred and upwards, attacked the house of the Rev. John Whitty of *Providence*. There were in the house at the time 15 Proteſtants of the Slieumargue cavalry—theſe brave fellows withſtood the fury of the enemy: for upwards of two hours they kept up an inceſſant fire from the windows, which galled the aſſaſſins very much. The firing from within having ceaſed, the rebels concluded the ammunition was expended, and were proceeding to ſet fire to the hall door, by means of ſeveral loads of ſtraw brought thither for that purpoſe, when they were fruſtrated by the intrepidity of Mr. Whitty who leaped out of a parlour window, ſhot two fellows in the act of fanning the ſtraw—a third on approaching Mr. Whitty met the ſame fate. Mr. W. jumped into the parlour window, exclaiming " the rebelly aſſaſins never made a ball to kill me."

I ſhould not omit informing you of the conduct of Mr. Duigan whoſe name I have ſeen in your ‡ *Firſt Part* of this Narrative. Being appriſed of the attack on Mr. Whitty's houſe, he rode off to Stradbally, and made known the ſituation of his friends; when Lieut. Col. Fane with a party of the 4th dragoons, and ſome of the Stradbally yeomenry ſet off to relieve this ſmall garriſon at *Providence*: but the rebels prepared againſt a ſurpriſe, had fixed their out-poſts at all the contiguous avenues, by whom information was brought them of the approach of the army.

‡ *See* PART *the* FIRST, *page* 35.

They immediately retreated up to Cappalug-hill, setting fire to every proteſtant houſe in their way, leaving 15 dead, and a great quantity of pikes. Numbers muſt have been wounded.

The ſufferers who eſcaped from their habitations (ſet on fire), experienced a ſafe aſylum, and every poſſible attention, from Peter Gale, Eſq; of Aſhfield, to whoſe houſe they flocked in numbers—men, women, and children.

The loyaliſts had one man killed (named Furney), going expreſs to Stradbally: he was ſurrounded by a ſet of rebels, near Caſtletown-church, who piked him in a dreadful manner—he fought gallantly; eſcaped from them, and rode near a mile, when he fell from his horſe, and expired near the avenue gate of Coolancull. (His brother, J. Furney, was wounded from a ball that grazed his face). Had he uſed the ſame precaution of his comrade, named Empy, who nearly met the ſame fate, he probably might have ſurvived.—He lay fainting on the road with the loſs of blood—having aſked ſome women for water to drink, which they refuſed; he then begged of them, for God's ſake, to ſend for a prieſt, that he was dying; they immediately brought him in, and adminiſtered every relief in their power, by which means he recovered.

Yours, &c.

FRENCH

# FRENCH INVASION,

### AND

## SECOND INSURRECTION IN IRELAND.

REBELLION had almost been suppressed in Ireland, through the effectual means uniformly adapted throughout the kingdom, by order of government, which was likely to have been succeeded by peace and tranquillity, till intelligence of the arrival of a French force was circulated. This soon evinced to the loyalists that the expiring embers would again revive, if not immediately extinguished, as the sequel will fully prove. The blood-thirsty and rapacious disposition, which, previous to this, had marked with the strongest traits of barbarity, the ferocious character of an internal foe; and which conducted them forward to commit, on those who had the misfortune to fall into their clutches, such deeds of cruelty! of wanton cruelty! as human nature must shudder at the recital of, again roused and called forth into action, those brave fellows, who, under *Divine* aid, proved the SAVIOURS OF IRELAND.—To them were addressed the following lines here introduced.

POEM,

## POEM.

### TUNE—RULE BRITANNIA.

AGAIN to seek our emerald isle,
  The frantic Gaul directs his way;
Even now his feet the land defile,
  Even now I hear sad ERIN say,
    " Once more arise ye patriot band,
    " Avengers of your native land."

### II.

" By all the fields your fathers won,
  " By all the blood yourselves have shed,
" Let every sire exhort his son
  " To emulate the mighty dead:
    " Then shall arise the patriot band,
    " Avengers of their native land.

### III.

" By Wexford's bridge begrim'd with blood,
  " The scene of many a murderous day,
" While silver Slaney's trembling flood
  " Ran blushing crimson to the sea!
    " To vengeance rise, ye patriot band,
    " To vengeance for your native land.

### IV.

" By Enniscorthy's blood-stain'd hill,
  " Where many a loyal hero lies,

                      " By

" By Ross's streets and Fowkes's mill,
" Once more, my sons, to glory rise;
" 'Tis ERIN calls her patriot band,
" Avengers of their native land.

V.

" By the sad matron's piercing screams,
" That mingle with her childrens' cries;
" From Scullabogue's detested flames,
" And claim their vengeance from the skies.
" 'Tis ERIN calls her patriot band,
" Avengers of their native land."

VI.

Yes, by those *gory fields* we swear,
By every immolated friend,
The loyal banner still to rear,
Our King and Country to defend.
Since ERIN calls her patriot band,
Avengers of their native land.

---

## LETTER XXIII.

KILLALA, OCTOBER 2, 1799.

Sir,

WERE I to attempt a detail of each occurrence relative to the landing of the French at this place, until they were forwarded to Dublin (by the canal), together with the proceedings and fate of the infatuated rebels who joined them, I

fear

fear it would be found too prolix for your present purpose. You say you have pledged yourself to the nation, to be *minute* in your SECOND PART—the following, I hope, will serve your purpose and afford satisfaction.

Yours, &c. D. T.

AMIDST all the horrors of the rebellion (the subject of your Narrative,) previous to the French invasion, this province (Connaught), happily for us, proved tolerably quiet—nor should we, I suppose, have been otherwise, but for the landing of the French, on the 22d of August, 1798, from three frigates and a brig, to the number of 1000 at least, near Killala, under Gen. Humbert, § with a number of officers, and some pieces of artillery. They immediately proceeded for this town—defeated and took prisoners a party of the P. of Wales's fencible infantry, commanded by Lt. Silles, who with a few of our yeomen-cavalry, boldly attempted to stop their progress; three or four loyalists were killed. The French lost no time in making themselves masters of Killala—

§ *General Humbert was accompanied in this expedition by some disaffected Irishmen, who had received commissions in the French service; some of whom afterwards forfeited their lives—a just punishment for their base treachery.*

the

the Bishop's palace was surrounded by the French, and a number of rebels, some in an uniform provided by their *new friends*. Nothing could exceed the consternation which prevailed throughout the town—the loyalists every moment expecting to be butchered in cold blood; men, women, and children drowned in tears, attempting to escape, but in vain! Every avenue leading from Killala, was thronged by rebels making in to receive the *fraternal embrace*, whose eyes indicated the malignity of their hearts—no one was permitted to depart, but on business which concerned the *invaders*. The Bishop of Killala, Dean Thompson, Dr. Ellison, and some other clergymen, with their families, were taken prisoners and confined to the Bishop's palace, but were all treated extremely well by the French officer commanding.

The following printed DECLARATION was profusely strewed throughout the streets, and read with avidity by their ignorant dupes.

## LIBERTY, EQUALITY, FRATERNITY, UNION!

IRISHMEN,

YOU have not forgot Bantry Bay—you know what efforts France has made to assist you. Her

affection

affections for you, her desire for avenging your wrongs, and enfuring your independence, can never be impaired.

After feveral unfuccefsful attempts, behold Frenchmen arrived amongft you.

They come to fupport your courage, to fhare your dangers, to join their arms, and to mix their blood with yours in the facred caufe of liberty! They are the forerunners of other Frenchmen, whom you fhall foon infold in your arms.

Brave IRISHMEN, our caufe is common; like you, we abhor the avaricious and blood-thirfty policy of an oppreffive government; like you, we hold as indefeafible the right of all nations to liberty; like you, we are perfuaded that the peace of the world fhall ever be troubled, as long as the Britifh Miniftry is fuffered to make with impunity a traffic of the induftry, labour, and blood of the people.

But exclufive of the fame interefts which unite us, we have powerful motives, to love and defend you.

Have we not been the pretext of the cruelty exercifed againft you by the Cabinet of St. James's? The heartfelt intereft you have fhewn in the grand events of our revolution—Has it not been imputed to you as a crime? Are not tortures and death continually hanging over fuch of you as are barely suspected of being our friends? Let us unite, then, and march to glory.

*We swear the most inviolable respect for your properties, your laws, and all your religious opinions. Be free; be masters in your own country. We look for no other conquest than that of your liberty—no other success than yours.*

The moment of breaking your chains is arrived; our triumphant troops are now flying to the extremities of the earth, to tear up the roots of the wealth and tyranny of our enemies. That frightful Colossus is mouldering away in every part. Can there be any Irishman base enough to separate himself at such a happy conjuncture from the grand interests of his country? If such there be, brave friends, let him be chased from the country he betrays, and let his property become the reward of those generous men who know how to fight and die.

Irishmen, recollect the late defeats which your enemies have experienced from the French; recollect the plains of Honscoote, Toulon, Quiberon, and Ostend; recollect America, free from the moment she wished to be so.

The contest between you and your oppressors cannot be long.

Union! Liberty! the Irish Republic!—such is our shout. Let us march. Our hearts are devoted to you; our glory is in your happiness.

The principal French officers continued in the palace—the remainder of the force were diftributed throughout the houfes: the French were very folicitous to be fupplied with the very beft provifions, and we found it our intereft to grant them all they required for to fecure our lives, daily threatned by the rebels. That they attempted the deftruction of the loyalifts wherever an opportunity offered is publicly acknowledged, even by *Gen. Humbert* in his letter to the prefident of the court martial before whom the traitor *Teeling* was tried; in endeavouring to exculpate him he afferts " Teeling by his bravery and gene-
" rous conduct has prevented in *all* the towns
" thro' which we have paffed the *infurgents* from
" proceeding to the moft cruel exceffes"—Yes my friend, the extirpation of *all* who profeffed themfelves inimical to their diabolical meafures, was invariably to have been adapted.

The veffels which brought our unwelcome guefts failed from Killala the 24th—probably they were intended to be employed on a fecond expedition. It will be readily admitted that our fituation during the time of our captivity was very alarming;—ignorant of the ftate of the Kingdom, expofed to the infults of the rebels—concluding from the accounts in hourly circulation, that the government had been overturned—alfo that an additional French force would immediately arrive,

tive, we would have preferred natural death to such a state of suspense.

Such was the encreasing insolence and thirst for our blood, that the prisoners in the palace could only have escaped the rebels by receiving arms, &c. from the officer commanding at the palace.—This you will meet in the official bulletin to which I refer you, Sir, for a faithful account of our deliverance.

---

DUBLIN CASTLE, 28th SEPTEMBER, 1798.

*Extracts of Letters from Major General Trench, to Captain Taylor, private Secretary to his Excellency the Lord Lieutenant, dated Camp, near Killalla, the 24th and 26th instant.*

Sir,

"I have the honor to acquaint you, for the information of his Excellency the Lord Lieut. that previous to my leaving Castlebar on Saturday the 22d instant, I had ordered Lord Portarlington with the regiment under his command, forty of the 24th light dragoons, Captain O'Hara's, Captain Wynne's, and Captain Crofton's corps of yeomenry, to meet me at Ballina, at ten o'clock on Sunday morning from Sligo. I also ordered the Armagh millitia, consisting of above three hundred men, under Major Acheson, to proceed from Foxford, and to o-operate with me me at the same hour. I marched with the Roxburgh light dragoons, three hundred of the Downshire, the Kerry regiment, the Prince of Wales's fencibles, and two curricle guns, with the Tyrawly cavalry, by the Barhague road, and ordered Colonel Fraser, with three hundred of his regiment, to march from Newport, where I had detached him on Friday, in order if possible, to cut off the retreat of the rebels. The forces under Lord Portarlington had been frequently attacked on their march, and Major Acheson was attacked by a large body of Rebels at Foxford. On every occasion they have been dispersed with slaughter.

On my arrival at Ballina, I found that the town had been evacuated by the rebels, and was occupied by the forces under Lord Portarlington, I immediately marched, without halting, for this place. At about two miles from the town our advanced guard was fired upon by that of the rebels. Finding that Ballina was in our possession, and hearing that the rebels had retreated to Killala, I ordered the Kerry regiment of militia, with the detachment of the 24th light dragoons, the Tyrawly, and Captain Wynne's corps of yeomen cavalry, to proceed by a forced march to Killala, by Rappa, which they performed with zeal and dispatch, as they entered the town at one end as our advanced guard entered it on the other, and maintained a quick and well directed fire on the rebels, who fled in all directions.

The officers and men under my command, behaved with zeal, spirit, and activity; and I feel myself much indebted to their exertions. I derived much advantage from fifty men of the Downshire regiment of militia, trained by Major Matthews as sharp shooters, and who, under his command, with a party of the Roxburgh light dragoons, formed my advanced guard. To Lieut. Col. Elliot, who, with forty of the Roxburgh, charged through the town, I feel much indebted. I must also beg leave to mention, in a particular manner, the assistance which I derived from Mr. Ormsby, of Gortnoraby, who, by his accurate knowledge of the country through which I passed, and its inhabitants, was of the greatest service. I also owe much to Mr. Orme, of Abbytown, and several other gentlemen in the neighbourhood of the disturbed country.

Upon entering the town of Killala, I proceeded to the palace of the bishop, who I much feared had suffered from the rage of the rebels, but was happy to find him and his family in safety, but preserved from their violence only by the authority which Charost, the French commandant of the town, possessed over them, but which was beginning rapidly to decline before we arrived,

arrived, infomuch, that he was obliged to arm himfelf, and the other French officers, with a number of carbines, which he delivered up loaded in his room: the bifhop, his family, and fervants, were armed in the like manner, by him, and ferved out with ammunition, in order to protect them from the threatened violence of the rebels. At the palace, the head-quarters of the commandant, I found two hundred and feventy barrels of powder.

Having heard late on the night of the twenty-fourth inft. that the rebels were affembling in great numbers at a place called the Lacken, I marched on the morning of the twenty-fifth in that direction; they fled and difperfed on our approach, but, by the activity of the men, feveral were overtaken, between fifty and fixty were killed, all in arms, and five taken prifoners. Amongft the killed were feveral in French uniforms. I did not return here till nine o'clock laft night. The men bore a fatiguing march of fourteen hours with zeal and fpirit. Bellew and Burke were hanged yefterday, by the fentence of a general court-martial. Five men came in and furrendered their arms this morning, under the proclamation; I truft that their example will be followed by many others.

P. S.

P. S. In our different actions with the rebels they loſt between five and ſix hundred men. We loſt but one man.

J. TRENCH,<br>*Major of Brigade.*

That our *viſitors* were prepoſſeſſed in behalf of the loyaliſts, and particularly of the Biſhop of Killala and thoſe confined with him in his palace, is evident from General Humbert's letter, which I doubt not but you will concur is worthy of being recorded in your NARRATIVE. It is as follows:

## TO THE LORD BISHOP OF KILLALA.

DOVER, OCTOBER 26, 1798.

*My Lord,*

On the point of returning to France, I think it incumbent on me to teſtify in a particular manner, the ſentiments with which you have uniformly inſpired me.

From the moment that I had the opportunity of being acquainted with you, I ceaſed not to regret that chance, and my duty as a ſoldier, obliged me, by carrying the ſcourge of war into your neighbourhood, to diſturb the domeſtic felicity which you enjoyed, and to which you were every way entitled—I fhould be happy indeed, if on my return to my country, I might flatter myfelf that I had acquired fome pretenfions to your efteem. Independently of the particular reafons I have for loving and refpecting you, the defcription that citizen Charoft has given me of all your acts of goodnefs to him and his officers, as well before as after the retaking of Killala, muft for ever claim from me the tribute of efteem and gratitude. I beg the favour of your Lordfhip to accept this acknowledgement of it, and to fhare it with your valuable family.

I am, with the higheft refpect,<br>My Lord,<br>Your moft humble fervant,<br>HUMBERT.

You may eafily conceive the happinefs that fucceeded upon our being liberated—joy fparkled from every loyal countenance—thofe who had undergone fo painful a feparation, now felt the felicity of the reftoration of their friends, whofe lives were for fome time doubtful. To HIM who brought to nought the machinations of thofe who rofe up againft us, be the eternal praife.

I am, Sir, &c.

THE

THE Editor flatters himself the following Account will afford to the Reader the information so long sought for, relative to *Castlebar*. It is extracted from the Journal of a Gentleman of great veracity, who favoured the Editor with the same, for this NARRATIVE.—The Statement will prove irrefragable.

———

ON the twenty-second of August, 1798, as we were going to bed, a yeoman of Ballina made through Foxford, shouting "Why are you going to bed, and the French in Killala?" Some mocked, and others cursed him, but I persuaded the men to arise, arm themselves, and not doubt it. At eleven o'clock that night, Dr. King, who fled to us from Ballina, confirmed it. He said there had been some strangers observed at Ballina for some days past; that three large frigates were seen by himself, which at first appeared with English colours—they had taken a fishing-boat and detained the men. About day break, a few troops of the Carabineers, and some yeomen went through Foxford, which were nearly as posted as picquets that night, between Ballina and Killala. Our men let their horses feed, taking the bits out of their mouths, and before they were mounted they were nearly surrounded
th

they retreated into Ballina, hanged on the crane a man caught foraging for the French, and then retreated into Castlebar; having lost the Rev. Mr. Fortescue, and some of their men, in the skirmish.

I returned to Castlebar that morning.—Expresses flew, and troops teamed in with us from that till Sunday following: Generals Hutchinson and Trench were in Castlebar, and General Taylor in Foxford.

On Sunday night, at ten o'clock, the Longford militia marched in; while eating some bread and cheese a shot was fired out of a window at them! O my friend, think of our situation! In the dark of the night; four thousand enraged soldiers in the town. A noise arose, the clamour of irritated passions! Arms clashed against each other, and glass flew from windows, whilst the enraged men called for vengeance on the culprit.—The General shouted for the officer commanding, (Captain Chambers) to stand in the street until the affair should be over. The fellow who fired the shot fled off, when he thought he had kindled a flame which would destroy the town. I am told if there had not been instant peace the General would have caused the cannon to be brought to bear on the street, and sweep it with grape-shot: but glory to the Prince of Peace, he gave us a silent street in ten minutes. The men had

had orders that night, to be mounted and fit for action at two in the morning. There were two roads between Catllebar and Killala, one called Foxford, and the other Bernanaguidha; on the former our troops were pofted, but on the latter our picquets met the French army, at two o'clock in the morning and narrowly efcaped being taken: they rufhed into the town, others were fent out, but returned with precipitation; the General was told the French were within fix miles of us at five in the morning.

On Monday about fix in the morning, fome of our troops went to Foxford the wrong road. Having requefted Capt. Chambers to accept my bed, I fat up all that night, drew a map of the country and fent it to the General. A little before day my wife told me, " I will fee this battle in the ftreet, having in a dream beheld Flags;—a green, and another of a different colour."—We then agreed to confult the bible— I firft opened for our army, 2 Kings, vii. 7. " Wherefore they arofe and fled in the twylight, " and left their tents, and their horfes, even the " Camp as it was, and fled for their life."—We opened next for our country, Jer. v. 15, " Lo " I will bring a nation upon you from far, O " houfe of Ifrael, faith the Lord; it is a mighty " nation, it is an ancient nation, a nation whofe " language though knoweft not, neither under-
" ftandeft

"ſtandeſt what they ſay."—I next opened for our King, pſal. lxi. 7, "He ſhall abide before God for ever, O prepare mercy and truth which may preſerve him."—I laſtly opened for my wife and myſelf, John xiii. 7, "Jeſus anſwered and ſaid unto him, what I do thou knoweſt not now, but thou ſhalt know hereafter."—From all theſe I concluded we ſhould loſe *that* battle, but that the King and Conſtitution would be ſtill upheld.

### BATTLE OF CASTLEBAR.

At 7 o'clock the French army was within a mile and an half of the town: our Infantry went out, and the lines were formed. When the French General viewed our lines, he ſcattered his Frenchmen in parties thin in the front, but covered them deep behind with the rebels in French uniforms, and drove them on with a ſtrong reſerve of Frenchmen and officers, and behind all, a vaſt multitude of plunderers, terrible to behold! eſpecially as a miſt lowered on the mountains behind them, which concealed their true force from our Generals—we ſtood in the ſtreet with trembling expectation, whilſt Generals, Aid-de-camps and officers ruſhed up and down in dread commotion. I then retired, and aſcended to a high window, from whence I ſaw our lines in action. O how I felt for the brave Highlanders,

Highlanders, who formed the left wing of our army; they, planted on a high hedge at the weſt end of the town, ſupported a conſtant fire until the French advanced near the points of their bayonets; the Highlanders were then forced to leave their poſt, and retreat in confuſion towards us. Col. Miller ruſhed into the town, crying, "Clear the ſtreet for a ſtreet action;" when in a moment, as a dam burſting its banks, a mixture of ſoldiers, of all kinds, ruſhed into the town at every avenue; a ſerjeant deſired that all the women ſhould go to the barrack, but Dr. Hennins, another family and mine, retired into a houſe, fell on our knees, and there remained in prayer until the town was taken.

There were men in our brigade of the higheſt valour, for inſtance Captain Chambers, he fought backward and killed a field-officer (it is thought a general); he found a muſquet in his way, which he exchanged with a trooper for a lighter; with this he fought on the bridge, until he killed five Frenchmen; he was then cloſely engaged with a French muſqueteer, when another Frenchman ran a bayonet down the Captain's throat, and drove the point of it out at the ſide of his neck; he fell, and nearly bled to death, when the rebel wantonly leaped on him, tore his clothes off, and robbed him of ſeveral guineas. On the other hand, the French fought moſt deſperately.—One of them received a ball in the fword-arm, he changed his fword and fought on—he then received a ball in the left breaft, but fought on; at length, a royal foldier plunged his bayonet through him. Now the royal troops grew furious! Many had their wives in the town, and would rather die than fly. Four brave highlanders at a cannon, kept up a brifk fire on the French; but were killed while loading, the gunner taken, and the guns turned on our men. Now the street-action became hot—before it was *peal* anfwering *peal*, but now *thunder* anfwering *thunder;* a black cloud of horrors hid the light of heaven—the meffengers of death groping their way as in gloomy hell, whilft the trembling echos which fhook our town, concealed the more melancholy groans of the dying! When they approached the new jail, our centinel (a Frafer fencible) killed one Frenchman, charged and killed another; fhot a third and a fourth, and as he fired at and killed the fifth, a number rufhed up the steps, dafhed his brains out, tumbling him from his ftand and the centry-box on his body. Still part of the French purfued our men; feven of them followed thirty-eight fome diftance, though our men killed the whole without any lofs on their part. One of thefe feven Frenchmen had his head divided by a fabre; a woman afked him in French would he be taken to fome place, "No," said

said he, "I will never leave this until the Devil takes me," and continued calling for beer until he died.—For near an hour the street action continued, when the French drum informed us we were to receive our conquerors. The command of temper evinced by these licensed plunderers of the world was truly amazing.—My wife fell on her knees (she was at the down-lying) entreating one of them to spare my life, he raised her up as a nurse would an infant saying, " *vive* :" but they demanded beef, bread, wine and beer; we purchased their favor as far as in our power, but the hand of God wrought secretly for us; six or seven of the Frenchmen continued with me while they were in Castlebar. The rebels who came in with them plundered, drank and robbed without feeling—They carried off my wearing apparel, of which I acquainted the Frenchmen, who handled them so roughly as to prevent a further repetition of such villainy.

The French and Rebels plundered Lord Lucan's and several other houses, the sight of them was truly terrible!—Multitudes flocking from all parts carrying their flags and shouting for " Liberty." Droves of sheep, cows and horses driven in every day—next the *tree of liberty* and an harp without a crown, are borne in triumph through the streets, followed by the common shouts " Erin go braugh."—Now the church is attacked,

attacked; obscene figures made on the pews, and some were so vile as to abuse in the most filthy manner the Bible and *table of the Lord!*—they called the Bible "the Devil's book"—Teeling told a lady; "he hoped that book of riddles would "soon be universally despised."—The next subject in dispute is the massacre of the Protestants— for three days this contest held. Teeling, a priest Kane, and some others carried the point in *our* favor. Mr. Kane reasoned thus, as I am informed: "Gentlemen when you were in the power "of the Protestants, they did not shed your "blood; when your friends were taken in Wex-"ford they were not put to death, but pardoned, "and take care you be not shortly in the power "of Government—finally, if you will massacre "the Protestants, put me to death with them.

The following proclamation was handed about to the deluded rebels.

## ARMY OF IRELAND.

### *LIBERTY, EQUALITY.*

*Head-quarters at Castlebar, 14th Fructidor, 6th year of the French Republic, one and indivisible.*

GENERAL Humbert, commanding in chief the Army of Ireland, being desirous of organizing, with as little delay as possible, an admini-
strative

strative power for the province of Connaught, directs as follows:

1st. The seat of the government shall be at Castlebar, until further orders.

2d. The government shall be formed of 12 members, who shall be named by the commander in chief of the French army.

3d. Citizen John Moore\* is appointed president of the government of the province of Connaught, and is specially entrusted with the nomination and the uniting of its members.

4th. The government shall immediately attend to the organization of the militia of the province of Connaught, and to the supplies for the French and Irish armies.

5th. Eight regiments of infantry of 1200 men each, and four regiments of cavalry of 600 men each, shall be organized.

6th. The government shall declare all those to be rebels and traitors, who having received arms, or clothing, shall not within 24 hours rejoin the army.

7th. Every individual, from the age of 16 to 40 inclusive, is required in the name of the Irish Republic, instantly to repair to the French camp, in order to march in mass against the common enemy, the tyrant of Ireland—the English;

\* *Afterwards taken prisoner by Colonel Crawford.*

whose destruction alone can insure the independence and the welfare of antient Hibernia.

(Signed)
The General commanding in chief,
HUMBERT.

How far the two following letters of General Humberts will be found correct I am not competent to determine; as they have however appeared in print, they cannot I presume subject your publication to censure: they also may be found interesting—the reader by consulting the various accounts given will be enabled to form an opinion of their validity.

## ARMY OF IRELAND.

*Head Quarters at Castlebar, 6th Year of the French Republic.*

*The General commanding in Chief the Army of Ireland, to the Executive Directory.*

I AM to report to you, Citizens Directors, what have been my operations in Ireland.

On the 4th Fructidor, as soon as I got within sight of Broadhaven, the army received the appellation of Army of Ireland. The wind being unfavourable, we could not make the land on that day.

On the 5th, the division of frigates, after beating against wind and tide during 12 hours anchored in the bay of Killala about three o'clock P. M. In confequence of our having hoifted the Englifh flag, many perfons of note, and fome Englifh officers, came on board ;—it is impoffible to defcribe their aftonifhment at the fight of us. At four orders were given to difembark. The Adjutant General Sarazin landed firft, at the head of the grenadiers. I ordered him to march to Killala, which he carried with the bayonet. I appointed him General of Brigade on the field of battle. The enemy was completely defeated. Of 200 men who defended the poft, about 20 only efcaped over the walls—the reft were taken or killed. Almoft all the prifoners begged to be permitted to ferve with us, and I readily confented to their requeft. The difembarkation was compleated towards 10 o'clock at night.

On the 6th, General Sarazin reconnoitred Ballina: a flight fkirmifh only took place, the enemy's cavalry having retired in full gallop the fpace of two leagues.

On the 7th, I marched with the army againft Ballina. General Sarazin at the head of the grenadiers and of one battallion of the line, difperfed every thing that oppofed his paffage. The Adjutant General Fontaine was directed to turn the enemy's flank. This attack fucceeded, and

he

he took several prisoners. I pursued the cavalry during a considerable time, with the brave 3d regiment of Chasseurs a Cheval.

On the 8th the French army was joined by a corps of United Irishmen, who were armed and clothed on the spot. Towards three o'clock P. M. I moved forward to Rappa, and remained in that direction until two o'clock A. M.

On the 9th, the army advanced to Ballina, where it took post, but marched from it at three o'clock P. M.—After a march of fifteen hours I arrived on the 10th, at six o'clock in the morning on the heights in the rere of Castlebar. Having examined the enemy's position, which was very strong, I ordered General Sarrazin to commence the attack. The enemy's out-posts were rapidly driven in, and were pursued as far as the foot of the enemy's position. The grenadiers charged their line of battle, and were supported by the infantry of the line. The columns deployed under the fire of 12 pieces of cannon. General Sarazin ordered the enemy's left to be attacked by a battallion of the line, which was obliged to give way, having received the fire of upwards of 2000 men. General Sarrazin flew to its support at the head of the grenadiers, and repulsed the enemy. The English during half an hour, kept up a tremendous fire of musquetry, to which General Sarrazin forbid reposting.

Our

Our determined countenance disconcerted the English General, and as soon as the whole of the army had come up, I ordered a general attack to be made. General Sarrazin drove in the enemy's right, and took three pieces of cannon. The Chief of Battalion, Ardouin, obliged his left to retire to Castlebar.

The enemy having concentrated his force in Castlebar, and protected by his artillery, kept up a terrible fire—but by a successful charge of the third regiment of chasseurs a cheval, made through the main street of Castlebar, he was forced to retire across the bridge. After several very destructive charges, both of cavalry and infantry, directed by General Sarrazin and Adjutant-general Fontaine, the enemy was driven from all his positions, and pursued for the space of two leagues.

The enemy's loss amounts to 1800 men (of which 600 were killed or wounded, and 1200 prisoners), ten pieces of cannon, five stand of colours, 1200 firelocks, and almost all his baggage. The standard of his cavalry was taken in a charge by General Sarrazin, whom I named General of Division on the field of battle. I also, during the action, appointed the Adjutant-general Fontaine, general of brigade, and the Chiefs of battalion Azemare, Ardouin, and Dufour, chiefs of brigade. I further named Captain Durival a

commander

commander of squadron, and Captains Toussaint, Zilberman, Ranou, Huette, Babiu, and Kutz, chiefs of battalion. I beg, Citizens Directors, that you will be pleased to confirm these promotions, and that you will send the commissions as soon as possible, as it will be productive of very good effects.

Officers and soldiers have shewn prodigies of valour. We have to regret the loss of some excellent officers and very brave soldiers. I shall very shortly forward to you further details; at present I will only add, that the enemy's army, consisting of between five and six thousand men, of which six hundred are cavalry, has been completely dispersed.

Health and respect,

(Signed) HUMBERT.

## ARMY OF IRELAND.

*Head Quarters, Castlebar, Sixth Year of the French Republic.*

*The General commanding in chief the Army of Ireland, to the Minister of Marine.*

I TRANSMIT to you, Citizen Minister, the copy of my letter to the Executive Directory. You will perceive that no exertions are wanting on on our part to fulfil the intentions of Government.

I have made several appointments, according to the actions and to the military talents displayed by those whom they regard, and I solicit your support in obtaining from the Executive Directory a confirmation of them.

About six hundred United Irish joined me on the 8th Fructidor, and were immediately armed and clothed. On the 10th they came forward to the heights in the rear of Castlebar. The first cannon shot that was fired drove them off. I expected as much, and their panic in no way deranged my operations.

The victory of Castlebar has produced excellent effects; and I hope within three days to have with me a corps of two or three thousand of the inhabitants.

The English army, which I yesterday defeated, is commanded by General Houghton, whose head quarters are now at Tuam. He intends to assemble twenty-five thousand men to attack me; and on my side I am doing my utmost to be well prepared for his reception, and even to go and meet him should circumstances justify such proceeding. We occupy Killala, Ballina, Foxford, Castlebar, Newport, Baliinrobe, and Westport. As soon as the corps of United Irishmen, which I wish to assemble, shall be clothed, I shall march against the

the enemy in the direction of Roscommon, where the partizans of insurrection are most zealous. As soon as the English army shall have evacuated the province of Connaught, I shall pass the Shannon, and shall endeavour to make a junction with the insurgents in the North. When this shall have been effected, I shall be in a sufficient force to march to Dublin, and to fight a decisive action.

The Irish have until this day hung back. The county of Mayo has never been disturbed, and this must account for the slowness of our progress, which in other parts would have been very different.

As this handful of French may possibly be obliged to yield to numbers, and that the noise of cannon may again produce on our new soldiers the effect it had at Castlebar, I desire you will send me one battalion of the third half brigade of light infantry, one of the tenth half brigade of the line, one hundred and fifty of the third regiment of chasseurs a cheval, and one hundred men of the light artillery; fifteen thousand firelocks, and a million of cartridges.

I will venture to assert, that in the course of a month after the arrival of this reinforcement, which I estimate at two thousand men, Ireland will be free.

The fleet may anchor in the bay of *Tarboy*, by 53, 55 latitude, south of *L'Isle Muttette*, and the disembarkation will be effected without difficulty.

I cannot sufficiently praise the conduct of the troops under my command. I must recommend my brave comrades to the gratitude of the nation, and to your paternal care.

Health and respect.<br>(Signed)     HUMBERT.

To account in part for our defeat at Castlebar, and also refute Humbert's pompous letter, it may not be improper (though not in the proposed order) to extract from a recent publication, the words of an officer serving under Lord Cornwallis, relative to the engagement at this place.

---

" THE French, with about fifteen hundred rebels, advanced in regular order upon the King's troops, who waited their approach in the position they occupied.‡ The artillery, under Captain Shortall, was admirably served, and made a visible impression, insomuch that the enemy's advance was actually checked, and they began to disperse: at this critical moment, our troops, as

‡ *See page* 217.

if seized with a sudden panic, and without any apparent reason, gave way; and notwithstanding every effort made by Lieutenant-general Lake, Major-generals Hutchinson and Trench, and the very meritorious exertions of all their officers, they could not be rallied, but retired in confusion through Castlebar, towards Hollymount. Lord Roden's fencible dragoons, however, shewed great gallantry upon this as they had upon all other occasions; they protected the retreat of the infantry, and even recovered a six-pounder which the French had pushed forward through Castlebar. The skeleton of the sixth regiment, under Major Macbean, also behaved with spirit in the action.

The following is the return\* of killed, wounded and missing, and of guns lost upon this unfortunate occasion. Of the soldiers of the Longford and Kilkenny militia returned missing, the greater part had deserted to the enemy. The loss of the French in killed and wounded (and resulting almost entirely from the effect of the artillery), was afterwards found to have been far more considerable than that of the King's troops."

\* *By comparing our return with Humbert's, page 226, the fallacy is notorious, and tends more fully to establish the French to excel in gasconading.*

The total of our lofs was, one ferjeant and fifty-two rank and file killed; two Lieutenants, three ferjeants, and twenty-nine rank and file wounded; two Majors, three Captains, fix Lieutenants, three Enfigns, two Staff, ten ferjeants, two drummers, and two hundred and fifty-one rank and file miffing—alfo nine field-pieces.

Caftlebar was nine days a republic; they elected a Mayor, two high Juftices and fix Municipal officers: *liberty, equality, fraternity* and *unity*, were their boafted profeffions!—Tho' we were flaves; was this *liberty?* the French eat bread and beef, drank wine and beer, giving the Irifh potatoes, and telling them to drink what they pleafed;—the French flept on *beds,* and the Irifh on *hay* in the fields; was this *equality?* the French beat and treated the rebels lik dogs; was this *fraternity?* and *they* fhot and murdered each other, was this *unity?* No; all was *democracy*!!! Next we were informed that every one who would not take up arms for the French fhould be put to death—then for the fecond time I refolved to meet death, and felt in profpect the fweets of martyrdom.—It has been reported that the French abufed women indifcriminately; but this is falfe—Many of us proved them both brave and generous—thofe who were lyons in the ftreet, feemed like lambs in the parlour—however I have imagined

this

this to be policy; and that if they had once conquered the country, they would in a mafs cut off all who had oppofed them: of this I am the more perfuaded, their firft tax upon Caftlebar being 2000 Guineas.—Cruel fpecimen of freedom. This is moft certain, the French mocked the Papifts, for paying any refpect to the Sabbath, not eating meat on Fridays, and wearing Scapulars, and in my own hearing they denied the refurrection.

Thus were we of neceffity fubject to this wild tyranny; had 2000 kings in our little town; women worfe than favages, bearing off hides, tallow, fuet, beef, and clothes of all kinds to the mountains—they even robbed and killed each other: a volume only would contain their unnatural acts. The day before they left us, the Marquis Cornwallis reached to Hollymount, fourteen miles from us, and on that night one of the Frenchmen who frequented my apartments came to me, told me the *Englifh* were coming, and that they muft depart; I then thought to meet them; but he meant to flee before them. On the ninth day they departed, commanding their commiffary and the mayor to have beef fufficient killed for them on their return. But they returned no more! And the Lord fent their fatal harpies and devouring locufts with them.

We remained in great diſtreſs, dreading their return all that day. Dr. Elliſon wrote a letter, and a young man, William Mayley, on my horſe (who was hid in a back kiln, and was five days without food or water); ventured to carry it to the Lord Lieutenant. The doctor finding the French were not returning, though he was their priſoner, ſet out when, near Hollymount, he met ſome Heſſians, Hanoverians, and Roxburgh fencibles, coming from the Marquis; with them he returned to Caſtlebar, at ten of a dark night. When our hope was nearly gone, we heard the noiſe of horſes, ran to the ſtreet, and heard the Heſſians (whom we ſuppoſed to be French) crying halloo! halloo! We remained ſilent, till Dr. Elliſon cried aloud, the "KING's TROOPS:" with grateful hearts we ſhouted "God ſave the King." Theſe brave men kept their ſaddles all night, though ſuch a heavy rain has been ſeldom experienced, and next day rode after the grand army, leaving us an hundred French priſoners, fifty of whom were able to fight: we had no other force than a few yeomen. In this fearful ſituation we remained, until Captain Norcott marched in with fifty-ſeven Fraſer fencibles;—thus we were obliged ſtill to continue in a ſtate of watching and terror for ſome nights.

On Wedneſday, September 12, before day-break, two of our men being ſtationed as picquets, Meſſrs.

Messrs. Edward Maley and John Dudgeon, they heard the noise of horses coming from the Gap, and proceeding to the road-side, demanded, "Who comes there?" Ans. "A friend." "A friend to whom?" Ans. "To the French." "O very well," said our heroes, "Come on, my lads, where are you going?" The rebels answered, "We are going to take Castlebar; we are captains, and there are two thousand coming within half a mile of us." Immediately these two brave loyalists closed in with them; one of them presented a pistol, the other his sword, saying " deliver your arms or you are dead men." Having made them prisoners, they entered the town shouting, " murder! murder! arise to arms, or you will be burned in your beds." This echoed so loud, all the town rung with it— hundreds repeated it;—men undressed rushed through the streets— incessant rain heavily descended! the drums beat " to arms, to arms," whilst the dark solitary walls re-echoed, "to arms, to arms!!! At last the tempest silenced the drum: but no cause could allay the vigilance of our townsmen, and the gallant handful of Frasers. The guards continued to bring in prisoners till morning.

At last welcome day shewn upon our afflicted town; to me it afforded much consolation, my wife being in the pangs of childbearing all night, tho' I thought will light save us? no! only serve to difplay our danger—thus hope and apprehenfion bent alternately the ballance. At length all our forebodings are confirmed by a difcovery of the plodding affaffins, planted to great advantage round the North-weft part of our devoted town. Capt. Norcott, with the fpirit of an Alexander commanded his few heroes to advance in order. Our defence that day againft 2000 armed rebels, (in a country all in rebellion and numbers in our town with open arms ready to receive them) confifted of 57 Frafers, 34 Townfmen and boys—and one corps of yeomen cavalry. The Frafer captain divided his men into four parts—one part by the only piece of cannon he had, at the market crofs—the fecond part he pofted in the center, between the markethoufe and the extreme entrance to the town—with the third part he covered half of the cavalry at the North end of the town, where he judged the rebels would attempt an entrance, and the fourth part he pofted in a Weftern-ftreet, near a bridge to cover the retreat of the 34 infantry, who were townfmen, chiefly volunteers in coloured clothes, and the other part of the cavalry he pofted on an eminence in the South end of the town oppofite the church.

The wifdom of Captain Norcott in this diftribution of his men appears, when we confider, firft, the Frafers were fo placed, that they defended

fended the town entrances—secondly, they were ready to save the cavalry from the pikes—thirdly, they could support the retreat of the 34 townsmen if overcome—fourthly they had such command of the interior of the street and goal, that our intestine foes could not stir; and fifthly all the Frasers could in a moment rush together, and assist each other if occasion required. I cannot say whether the captain had all this in view, but I could prove it all from the positions of his little Highland army. There was in the town at this time a certain gentleman who gave it as his advice to flee to Tuam, and leave our wives, children, sick and aged with our property to the savage plunderers—I mention this to correct a base news paper report which gave him the chief place in our deliverance—But thank God a Scotchman had the command—Captain Urquhart will be held in grateful remembrance by the loyalists of Castlebar.

*SECOND BATTLE OF CASTLEBAR.*

About 7 o'clock in the morning the firing commenced; the rebels were furious, and fired with determination and close direction, at length a Mr. John Gallagher rushed from his ranks upon the rebels and was followed by his brother who commanded the party—another party then flew on the enemy—the Frasers burned with ardour to be in the action; hence all pursue the flying banditti,

banditti, except a small detachment which re-mained with Lieut. Denham to keep poffeffion of the town—now the cavalry dart upon them, kill and take prifoners until they fill our goals—numbers attempting to crofs a river were drowned, and many found dead in a lake. One rebel prifoner brought in, (his neck torn by a ball and two lodged in his body,) confeffed that the intentions of that band were, to deftroy the Proteftants, man, woman and child—and to plunder the town, killing even the Loyal Papifts! Thus by divine mercy ended the fecond engagement at Caftlebar! It was awful to fee thofe harpies like rooks blackening the diftant hills as they afcended. After this Newport and Weftport were taken by the rebels, but * Capt. Urquhart with the Rt. Hon. D. Browne, re-took both.

---

THE Editor cannot fufficiently exprefs his gratitude to the very learned and intelligent Gentleman who favoured him with the following particulars relative to the rebellion in the counties of Cavan and Longford—he confiders them to be a defirable acquifition for this NARRATIVE, and participates in the fatisfaction they muft afford the reader.

\* *Errata—for Norcott, throughout the affairs of Caftlebar, read Urquhart.*

LETTER

## LETTER XXIII.

CAVAN, SEPT. 5, 1799.

*Sir,*

I HAVE met with so many things to engross me, that I have been obliged, very reluctantly, to delay the statement herewith sent, to this late hour. I am sorry it is not better executed—I can only say that it is faithfully and truly detailed, and you may depend upon its accuracy.

I remain, Sir,

Your obedient humble servant.

---

THE county of Cavan was one of those counties, in which the people, called *Defenders*, first made their appearance. So early as the beginning of the year 1794, their numbers and strength in that part of the kingdom were such, that they ventured to appear in arms in the day-time, and to face his Majesty's troops in two separate engagements! On one of those occasions they repulsed the City of Dublin militia more than once, at Ballinagh, and were preparing to advance against the town of Cavan, when the Dublin militia, aided by the Ballyduff armed association, attacked them again in the most gallant manner, forced their way into the town of of Ballinagh, and totally routed the army of the *Defenders*. Thus defeated, the *Defenders* did not afterwards venture again to meet in array in that neighbourhood in the day-time, but their nightly depredations spread terror and desolation throughout that county, even to the very streets of Cavan, where a strong garrison, composed of the Wexford militia, was posted. The alacrity and spirit, shewn by that regiment on those occasions, reflect the highest honor both on the officers and men. It was a matter of the most poignant reflection, that the *Defenders* invariably drew a line between the two religions—the PROTESTANT and the ROMAN-CATHOLIC; the former of whom was exclusively the object of attack.

The principles of the *United Irishmen* embraced a scheme of infinitely more extent, than that formed by the *Defenders*. The latter soon gave place to the former, or was included in it.— Treason sought not only to make proselytes amongst the loyal, but to embrace under its *green banners* every society, however infamous their members or their objects—" *Pete auxilium etiam ab infimis,*" said the Roman conspirator to his agents. The wretched half-naked peasant of the mountains, and the wealthy and substantial trader—the acred squire and the desperate spendthrift—the humble labourer and the titled Machiavelian—the atheist and the devotee—the Protestant,

Protestant, the Roman-Catholic, and the Presbyterian—the troops of the line—the militia of the country—the volunteer yeoman—the seaman and the marine—all, all were included within the system of *seduction*, and were alike the dupes of it. The gilded title-page, which prefaced their doctrines, imposed upon and misled many; the history of their proceedings and progress is too well known, and too deeply felt by the nation at large, as well as by individuals, to make a further statement of them now necessary.

In a former part of this work, a detail has been given of the *various actions which had taken place between his Majesty's troops and the rebel armies*, previous to the autumn of 1798. It would naturally be supposed that the numerous defeats which the rebels had every where experienced, would have been sufficient to have deterred them from any further efforts in the field; but the approach of foreign aid roused all their hopes, and animated them to fresh enterprises.

In the counties of Westmeath and Longford, and in parts of the counties of Cavan and Leitrim, the agents of the treasonable societies had been uncommonly successful in enlisting the lower orders of society under their banners; However, in the two latter counties, they had not been able to seduce any person of wealth or consequence to become a leader; but in the county

county of Longford they found many of that description, who were enthusiasts in their cause, and who influenced thousands by their example. Amongst these were Alexander and Hans Dennistoun, both of them men of property and respectability in the neighbourhood of Granard—the former of whom was the first Lieutenant in the Mastrim yeomen cavalry; and several other members of that corps, O'Hara, Cromie, and many more, also raised the rebel standard, and armed their followers against their king.

The last expedition prepared by the French republic against Ireland, was previously well known to the traitors in Belfast, and elsewhere. Hans Denniston was dispatched from the county of Longford to that town, to receive instructions. His return to the county of Longford was to be the signal for a general rising, in order to co-operate with and assist the French troops, who were then in the kingdom, and were advancing rapidly, and with whom the Longford rebels kept up a close communication from the moment of their landing. A strong post in a fertile part of the kingdom was deemed necessary to be secured for the French, in their progress to Dublin, and Granard, which lay in the circuitous route which the position of Lord Cornwallis's army obliged the French general to take, seemed to be such a post as was desired. Every thing was

was prepared for securing that place, by what they deemed an irresistable attack—Hans Denniston had returned from Belfast on the third of September—agents and emissaries were dispatched every where, to collect the rebel troops. Three thousand came from the county of Westmeath, and in their march they disarmed a part of the Mastrim corps, commanded by Captain Bond, several disaffected members of which joined the rebels. Great and shameful neglect was imputable to those whose duty it was, and who had full opportunity of warning Granard of its approaching danger; but either cowardice or disaffection withheld those persons from doing any act which might prove prejudicial to the rebel cause; and thus Granard remained unapprized of the approach of the enemy, till it was too late to prepare against it. Armies were organized in the counties of Monaghan and Cavan, and were ready to co-operate with the Longford rebels as soon as Granard had fallen—of which event no doubt was then entertained; and Cavan, where there was a considerable depot of arms and ammunition, was to be immediately attacked by the united rebel armies, whose numbers would then have been immense—Monaghan alone furnished twenty-three thousand men, who were armed, and ready to march to form a junction with the

Longford

Longford and Cavan rebels, as soon as Granard was taken.

The garrison of Granard was at that time very weak. The yeomen corps of that town, and a few of the Ballymacue corps, under Captain Pailes, were its only defence. On the night of the fourth of September, the rebels encamped within view of the place—on that day detachments from two of the county of Cavan corps were sent thither, consisting of twenty-five men of the Crossdoney infantry, and fifteen of the Kilmore corps; but this reinforcement could be of little service in resisting the threatened attack on Granard. In the night of that day, expresses were sent from thence to Major Porter, who commanded the Argyle fencible regiment, to send speedy relief. That regiment had arrived but a day or two before from Belfast at Cavan and Belturbet, by forced marches, in order to oppose the progress of the French, who were advancing from Castlebar. Major Porter, under the orders he had received, did not hold himself at liberty to detach any of his men from Cavan, which was a post of infinitely more importance than Granard; and conceiving that the appearance of the rebels before Granard might be only a feint to draw off or weaken the garrison of Cavan, and thereby expose it to a successful attack—he therefore

therefore for some time prudently declined to send any troops from thence; but further expresses continuing to arrive from Granard, at one o'clock, A. M. on the fifth, Major Porter consented that Captain Cottingham should march to its relief, with detachments of the Cavan and Ballintemple corps of yeomen infantry. The events of the fifth of September have been already laid before the public in the official letter written on the spot by Captain Cottingham, which letter is here transcribed.

GRANARD, SEPT. 6, 1798.

*My Lord,*

I HAVE the honor to state to your Lordship, that the rebels were yesterday defeated near this place with great slaughter.

Having received orders from Major Porter of the Argyle regiment, who commanded at Cavan, to proceed without delay with detachments from the Cavan and Ballintemple corps of yeomen-infantry, consisting of eighty-five men, to the relief of Granard, which was threatened by the rebels—I marched from Cavan at three o'clock in the morning of the 5th inst. with all possible expedition, and arrived between seven and eight at Granard—the rebel army was then in view of the town, in full march to it, armed with musquetry and pikes, amounting (as appeared by the testimony of several prisoners) to more than six thousand men, and commanded by Mr. Dennifton, a Lieutenant in the Maftrim cavalry, who, with others of that corps, and several respectable persons in that neighbourhood, had joined the rebel standard.

### BATTLE OF GRANARD.

The hill on which Granard is built, affording me a strong position, I there drew up under cover of a hedge at some distance from the town, my whole force, consisting only of one hundred and fifty-seven infantry, and forty-nine cavalry, and composed of the above detachments and those specified in the margin,* who had formed the garrison of that place. The rebels advanced in one column to attack us in front, but seeing the advantage which our situation gave us, and which protected our front, they halted, and after firing some shots at us, they formed themselves into three columns, the centre one of which was comparatively weak and irregular, and advancing slowly, was evidently intended merely to engage our attention, while the other two columns, which

---

* *Cavan infantry*, 53—*Ballintemple do.* 31—*Longford do* 9—*Croffdoney do.* 25—*Kilmore do.* 15 —*Ballymacue dismounted cavalry,* 24—*Total* 157.
 *Ballymacue cavalry,* 18—*Granard do.* 31—*Total* 49.

were

were of great strength, and formed in perfect military order, moved off to the right and left, under cover of a high hedge, for the purpose of gaining our flanks, and cutting off our communication with the town; this made it necessary that I should retreat to a second position nearer to Granard. The rebels having collected a vast number of cattle, and having goaded them with their pikes, drove them at this instant furiously against us, but we had the good fortune to be able, without being thrown into confusion, to turn them aside in another direction.

Our front being again protected by a bank, we waited the approach of the rebels, who trusting to the effect which they expected from the fury of the cattle, advanced close to our line, and were received by a fire so well directed and heavy, that they soon fell into disorder, and after some time began to give way in all points. This happy moment was seized, and the bayonet completed their defeat. The slaughter which ensued was great indeed—and would have been infinitely more so, had the nature of the ground been such as to have allowed the cavalry to act. It is impossible as yet to ascertain the number of the slain—but they greatly exceed four hundred men. Several leaders were killed, one of whom was the son of a gentleman of an ancient and respectable

table family, whofe only confolation now is, that he has expiated his treafon with his life.

The action continued with little interruption from a few minutes after nine till near three in the afternoon. One column of the rebel army fled over the mountains towards Mohill, and the other took its direction towards Edgeworthftown. I have the fingular happinefs to ftate, that on our part not a life was loft; and only two men were wounded, both of whom are recovering.

When it is confidered that the whole force which I had the honor to command on this occafion, confifted entirely of detachments from yeomenry corps, fo few in number, and without the aid of any regular troops, and oppofed to an enemy fo formidable by their numbers, I hope your Lordfhip and their country will think, that they have faithfully difcharged the truft repofed in them.

Were my tribute of praife of any value to the officers with whom I had the honour to act, I would have much to fay; but the event fpeaks a language ftronger than my pen can utter. It is a matter of real regret, that the exertions of the cavalry were fo feverely reftrained by the ftrength of the inclofures, which difabled them from adding that eclat to the action which their fpirit and zeal would otherwife have done. I cannot, however,

ever, omit my acknowledgements to Captain Palles, of the Ballymacue cavalry, and Captain Bell, and Lieutenant Helden of the Granard cavalry, for their anxious endeavours to contribute to the succefs of the day; to Lieutenants Erſkine and Armſtrong, of the Cavan infantry; Lieutenant Bell, of the Ballintemple infantry; Lieutenant Booth, of the Croſſdoney infantry; Lieutenant Bell, of the Ballymacue difmounted cavalry, and Moutray Erſkine, Eſq; who gallantly volunteered on this occaſion; and to the troops in general I can only ſay, that the hiſtory of the day will be the beſt comment on their conduct.

I have the honor to be, my Lord,
Your Lordſhip's moſt obedient ſervant,

J. H. COTTINGHAM,
*Capt. Cavan and Ballybaiſe infantry.*

To the particulars detailed in the above letter are ſuperadded a few more, which will aſſiſt in laying before the reader the fulleſt ſtatement of an action, the benefits reſulting from which were of an extent great beyond calculation.

When Captain Cottingham had taken up his poſition to receive the attack of the rebel army, the moat of Granard, and the barracks, were occupied by the Granard difmounted cavalry. The moat is a ſmall Daniſh fort, raiſed to a conſiderable

siderable height above the adjoining ground, and lately surrounded by a low parapet wall, by the Hon. Major Packenham, of the 23d light dragoons, who had been quartered there at the time of the French landing—within the fort is a very small brick building, which serves as a guard-room, and the whole fort is capable of containing about fifty men. It stands near the western entrance into Granard, on the highest point of the hill on which that town is built.— The barracks are at the eastern entrance into the town—they are surrounded by a high wall, on the four angles of which four small bastions have been erected. In this place Ralph Dopping, Esq; took post with a few men, and by his judicious and spirited conduct checked the left column of the rebels, which had attempted to enter at that end of the town, and had made a violent effort to take the barracks by assault.

During the whole of this memorable action, Captain Cottingham received the most essential assistance from Andrew Bell, Esq; of Drumkeel, in the county of Cavan, a member of the attornies cavalry, who though not attached to any corps engaged on that day, yet in the most spirited manner volunteered his services, and acted as aid-de-camp to Captain Cottingham during the heat of the action, and by the precision with which he delivered every order from the commandingmanding-officer, and by his own personal exertions, at a time when every individual had ample scope for individual exertions, is fully entitled to those acknowledgments, which Captain Cottingham has been heard to make, and which were omitted in the official account before transcribed, through the hurry and tumult which naturally took place at the time when that account was written—but the names of Mr. Dopping and Mr. Bell should not be now omitted, in a work, which has for one of its objects, not only the detail of gallant actions, but also that of being a memorial of those to whom their country became indebted in the moment of her distress.

The number of the slain on that day, far exceeded the amount stated in the official letter; we have authority to say it nearly doubled it. The defeat of the rebels was so complete, as well as so unexpected by them, that almost all their chiefs, who survived the action, fled in every direction, and every hope was blasted of again raising the standard of rebellion in that neighbourhood. This will fully appear, when it is told, that on the approach of the French to the town of Granard, on the eighth of September, not a single rebel was seen to raise his head in that neighbourhood.

The right column of the rebel army was by much the strongest; and was composed principally of of the rebels who had marched on the day preceding from the county of Weſtmeath. A large body of theſe moved off together, after their defeat, to Wilſon's-Hoſpital,† which they took poſſeſſion of, and were there preparing to butcher in cold blood, a number of Proteſtants, whom they had confined in ſome of the rooms; when Major Porter, who had marched from Cavan the evening after the action at Granard, fortunately arrived at the Hoſpital, with two hundred and fifty of his regiment, Captain Palles and his cavalry, and ſome other corps of yeomen-cavalry, who had joined him. After a ſhort but ſmart action, the rebels fled in every direction, and the wretched victims were reſcued from death at the very inſtant, when it was about to be dealt out to them in a manner the moſt ſavage.

The plans of the rebels were fully diſcovered. Had Granard fallen into their hands, of which they admitted no doubt, Cavan was on the next day to have been attacked by the Granard army, aided by above twenty-three thouſand men from the county of Monaghan alone; whilſt other rebel armies, which were fully organized, and ready to riſe at a moment's warning, were to fall on Belturbet and Killiſhandra. The weight of their immenſe numbers, fluſhed with victory, and inſpirited

---

† *Detailed in pages.* 254—263.

inspirited by the near approach of the French, would too probably have borne down the gallant troops, which defended those places. Had they fallen, the French would have been enabled to have thrown great and powerful obstacles in the way of the Marquis of Cornwallis and of General Lake: and the scenes of devastation and of murder, which a victorious rebel army would too surely have exhibited, would have rendered the North alike with the South—a dreadful example of the effects of rebellion.

Great and decisive therefore, were the benefits derived from this victory. The safety of the North, perhaps of Dublin too, was secured by it.

THE following is an authentic extract of a letter which was written without any intention of appearing in print, by a Gentleman of the highest character and respectability, since deceased, who narrowly escaped becoming the victim of his loyalty and humanity; it is here inserted—being preparatory to the attack at Wilson's hospital; for which see pages 258—263.

## LETTER XXV.

MULLINGAR, SEPT. 10, 1798.

*My Dear——*

THANK the Almighty God I now sit down in peace, to give a recital of some of the events which

which happened in this diſtrict, as far as I am able to recollect. On Tueſday, the fourth of September, a yeoman from near Newpaſs, came expreſs to let me know the country was *up* there; while he was making his report my ſervant came in, and informed me that the hills were covered with men: on this I prepared for defence, with four Proteſtants and two others, and ſtood to my arms all night. In the morning I received a letter from my neighbours, letting me know that neither my perſon or place ſhould be moleſted; I ſent for one or two of them, returned my thanks, told them I wiſhed to keep my arms to defend myſelf from plundering parties; they ſaid I ſhould, and deſired to ſee me at Bunbruſna. I went there, met ſome of their leaders who ſeemed willing to return to their buſineſs on an oblivion of what had paſſed, and requeſted that I would go to the commanding officer at Mullingar, and acquaint him of it.

As ſoon as I got home, an expreſs came after me, to let me know that the troops were marching to Multifarnam; I went there, among the acclamations of the people, and proceeded to meet them (the troops), but it proved a falſe alarm; on my return it was ſettled that —— and —— of Bunbruſna, ſhould go with me to Col. Blake, of the Northumberland fencibles, commanding-officer at Mullingar, from whom I
brought

brought the following anfwer obtained with difficulty: "Colonel Blake cannot enter into any engagement with perfons in arms againft their Sovereign, but in confequence of my reprefentation he fufpends the operation of the troops for a few hours, in expectation of an unconditional fubmiffion:" (this was a fimilar reply to that given by the juftices to complaints they made of grievances). We returned with the above anfwer from Colonel Blake, and found that Lord Longford had been at Multifarnam, and had taken the road to Lackin, in order to meet troops coming from Granard; I followed his Lordfhip, the order was enough for him; when I returned to them (the rebels), the alarm was given that there were troops on the road from Balnalack, which created a general confufion among them. Now begins the awful fituation in which I was for I believe half an hour;—I was to go and meet the troops, in order to poftpone the attack, conducted through the rebels (who were in general drunk) by fome of their leaders; we had not gone fifty yards along the wall from the Hofpital-gate ‡ until

‡ *Wilfon's-hofpital is a charitable Proteftant inftitution, for maintaining, &c. twenty aged men, and an hundred boys, fituated within a few miles of Mullingar, Co. Weftmeath. It was founded by* *Andrew*

until we were stopped by the people who lined it, presenting at us, swearing we should not pass, and were afterwards seized by others with pikes, pistols, &c. to our breasts, saying we would betray them, &c. &c. this happened two or three times, the same imprecations, &c. continuing, until at last a person came up, whom I addressed, begging if they did not chuse I should go, that I might be put in a place of safety: he seeming to have some authority went with me, and though often called to stop, conveyed me safe through them; immediately after which, I am told, another party followed to put me to death, but were prevented by some others, who would not suffer it. After this escape I got as far as the turn from Bunbrusna to my own house, and just as I was in the act of taking off my hat to ask for the commanding-officer, the field-pieces attached to the Argyle fencibles fired in my front three discharges, before I could get out of the line of the fire—and another man with me: but we fortunately escaped. Whether they were through mistake pointed at us or not I have not heard; I think not, but over our heads at the rebels, who probably appeared on the hill going to the Hospital. As soon as I

*Andrew Wilson, Esq; of Piersfield in said county, who bequeathed the principal part of his property towards its support.*

got

got clear I made my way to Mullingar, congratulating myself on what I believe you will allow to be a most providential escape, leaving the contending parties to determine the fate of the day.

Having given you a brief detail of the dangers by which I was encompassed, I shall inform you of ——‡ *hair's-breadth escape*—you must know that he passed through Bunbrusna, escorting an artillery-cart of ammunition, &c. the very morning of the rising; they were to convey it to Edgeworthstown, but as the commanding-officer refused to take it from them, though by the route obliged to take it, they marched on with it smartly, and shortly after they left Edgeworthstown it suddenly blew up; the explosion killed the two drivers and five horses, and wounded two yeomen very severely, as also a son of Mr. —— who I understand is likely to recover.

I now congratulate you on our having the French in our hands;—when they surrendered at Ballinamuck, and the rebels were given no quarters, I understand even their French friends fired on them and tumbled many.

Yours, most sincerely,

‡ *His son.*

## LETTER XXVI.

Mullingar, October 3, 1799.

Sir,

I received your favour, and shall be happy to give you every information in my power, relative to the late rebellion in Westmeath. The perusal of the First Part of your Narrative has afforded me much pleasure—the descriptions are very interesting—and it is pleasing to think, that the spirited exertions and glorious success of our brave loyalists, are to be handed down to posterity.

Wilson's-Hospital, is a very fine Protestant institution. It is situated about six miles from Mullingar, on the Longford side, and lies between the villages of Multifarnam and Bunbrusna. On Tuesday, the fourth of September 1798, in the middle of the day, a party of armed rebels, several of whom were the hospital labourers, ran into the house, with the intention of surprising the Rev. Mr. Radcliffe, who is chaplain and superintendant, and taking the arms. He happened to see them when they were near the door, and had just time to snatch a gun and run to meet them. This opposition, though unassisted, except by a servant boy who carried a blunderbuss for him, was for that day effectual; as the party thought proper to retreat without accomplishing their

their purpofe. In the fcuffle Mr. R. was very feverely wounded, and two of the rebel captains flightly.

On Wednefday, the fifth of September, at about feven o'clock in the morning, the hofpital was furrounded by a prodigious multitude of rebels, men and women, amounting on a moderate computation, to upwards of five thoufand. Their cry was for the arms, which Mr. R. being weak from the lofs of blood, and not having any one he could depend on, ordered to be delivered to them, on their promife of retiring peaceably. As foon, however, as they had got the arms, they broke in the doors with fledges, and plundered the houfe of many articles—they even took away the clothes of the old men and boys, and ftripped off their fhoes and ftockings. After they had plundered for an hour, they took Mr R. prifoner, and brought him to the village of Multifarnam, where he was liberated through the interpofition of Mr. Moran, the parifh-prieft. He was then fo fortunate as to get fafe into Mullingar, where he was confined by his wounds for eight weeks. The rebel army marched from Multifarnam to the crooked wood, five miles from the Hofpital, expecting to be joined there by great numbers from the county of Meath; they remained in the wood all the night of Wednefday the fifth, feafting on the fat fheep of the neighbouring gentry,

gentry, and drinking the wine, &c. which they had plundered from different houses. On Thursday morning they returned to Wilson's-Hospital, took possession of it as a barrack, and were joined by a large body from the county of Longford. Their numbers now amounted to upwards of seven thousand men, remarkably well armed, and so confident were they of victory, that they were frequently heard to defy the army of ten counties. The strength of their position was indeed very great, being surrounded by walls, thick hedges, and plantations. They had taken in the two preceding days, twenty-eight Protestant prisoners, who had not given them any other offence, except that of being *Protestants!* These unfortunate people were now hourly threatened with a cruel death; and as some of them have declared, were on the point of being led out to be butchered, when the report of a cannon at a little distance, threw the rebels into confusion.

Lord Longford, who had not been apprized of the rising till Wednesday the fifth, used most uncommon exertions to collect a force capable of opposing so large a body of rebels with some prospect of success; and was so fortunate as to join two corps of yeomenry to his own, one from Finnœ in the county of Cavan, and one from Oldcastle in the county of Meath. With this force, amounting in the whole, cavalry and infantry,

fantry, to something upwards of one hundred, his Lordship marched towards the Hospital, on Thursday the sixth; and near the village of Bunbrusna, at about four o'clock, P. M. was joined by a detachment of the Argyle fencibles, one hundred strong, with one field-piece, commanded by Major Porter. This detachment marched that morning from Granard, a distance of twelve miles, and met Lord Longford by appointment.

### BATTLE OF WILSON'S-HOSPITAL.

As soon as the rebels were convinced the army had arrived at this place, they sent five hundred of their stoutest men from the Hospital, armed with musquets and fowling-pieces, and a large body of pikemen, to attack them. The highlanders were at this time posted on the high road, near Bunbrusna, drawn up in very close order, with the field-piece in their centre.

A desperate party of rebels issued from the main body, and ran with violence towards the cannon, advancing almost to its muzzle, with a determination to seize it; but by a discharge of grape-shot, they were made to pay dearly for their temerity. At this time, two of the artillery-men were shot by a rebel from behind a hedge.

The infantry now, made so good a use of their musquets, that the rebels broke, and were pursued

sued by the cavalry in all directions. A large party fled to the hill of Laney, just by, and were overtaken by the yeomenry, who did great execution among them. Another party got into the house and offices of a wealthy farmer, on the Mullingar road, and from thence fired on the troops; the thatch taking fire from the wadding of the guns, the houses were consumed; and it was said, that several of the rebels were burned in them. Another party took shelter behind the demesne walls, and in the plantations of the Hospital, but were quickly dislodged by two or three discharges of grape-shot. *At the attack on the cannon,* one Barden, the leader, a rich miller, was heard to cry out, " Boys, seize the gun, and the day is your own; then twist your pikes in their Protestant guts, and tear their Orange souls out." Darkness coming on put a stop to the exertions of the military, who lay all night on their arms; the fencibles on the road, near the Hospital, and the yeomenry in a field behind it. In the middle of the night, a party of rebels stole unperceived within shot of the yeomenry, and discharged a volley at them, but without effect; Lord Longford's infantry returned the fire, and twelve men of the rebels were found dead in the morning. At break of day, on Friday the 7th of September, Major Porter supposing that the rebels were in possession of the Hospital,

Hospital, was preparing to batter it, when he was informed they had evacuated the place. The troops then marched into it, and refreshed themselves with wine, and beef and mutton ready dressed: a large quantity of provisions having been prepared for the French, who were expected by the rebels that day. All the black cattle and sheep which had been driven into the Hospital-demesne, were restored to their proper owners. The rebels were said to have lost in the engagement and pursuit, near two hundred in killed and wounded. Could the battle have begun two or three hours sooner, the slaughter would have been prodigious. Thousands threw away their arms, and fled in the greatest confusion, on the first report of the cannon, and never again returned to the scene of action.

The loss, on the part of the King's troops, was only the two artillery-men before-mentioned. Thus, under the direction of Providence, were seven thousand rebels well armed, and confident in their strength, routed by about two hundred loyalists, who had made a fatiguing march on the day of battle. At the time of the insurrection, the Northumberland fencibles, a fine regiment, lay at Mullingar, but were so weakened by sending detachments to different parts, that the commanding-officer thought his whole force barely

sufficient

sufficient for the defence of the town, which was much threatened.

Every circumstance that took place I give you on my own authority and that of respectable persons who were present; and I believe the account to be pretty accurate. I have written in a hurry, therefore hope you will be so good as to dress this up, and make what use you please of it.

I am, Sir,

Your obedient humble Servant,

T. R.

## LETTER XXVII.

### TO THE PUBLISHER.

HAVING seen many inaccurate accounts of the action sustained on the 5th inst. at Coolooney, by a detachment under my command, against the French and rebel army, I think it incumbent on me, in justice to the officers and soldiers, who served so gallantly on that occasion, to give a fair account of the business to the public; which I should have done before, but that I expected my official report would have appeared.

CHARLES VERREKER.
*Colonel Limerick City Militia.*

SLIGO, SEPTEMBER 30, 1798.

ABOUT

ABOUT nine o'clock in the morning of the fifth, Captain O'Hara, of the Liney yeomen-cavalry, who commanded my advanced piquet at Tubbercurry, reported to me that he had been driven back by the advanced guard of the enemy, after a smart skirmish, in which he had one man killed and another wounded. Shortly after, I learned that a division of the French army had arrived at Colooney, with an intention, as I conceived, of attacking this town, and as I judged it more adviseable to attack them than to wait to be attacked, I marched out with two hundred and fifty of the Limerick City militia, two curricle guns, twenty of the Essex fencible infantry, thirty yeomen infantry, and a troop of the 24th regiment of light dragoons.

*BATTLE OF COLOONEY.*

On coming near Colooney, I found the enemy posted on this side of the town, ready to receive me. I accordingly ordered Major Ormsby, with one hundred men, to occupy a hill which covered my right, my left being protected by a river. I then moved forward to the enemy, when a very close and severe action commenced, which lasted near an hour and an half; at length, the very superior number of the enemy enabled him to outflank the division on my right, which was compelled

compelled to fall back. At that time perceiving the enemy to make a difpofition to furround me, and my ammunition being nearly expended, a retreat became abfolutely neceffary.—From the unfortunate circumftance of one of the gun horfes being fhot in the act of harneffing, we were obliged to abandon our two field-pieces—but as our ammunition waggon, and the whole of the gun harnefs were preferved, the guns became ufelefs to the enemy, who, in confequence, left them behind.

Our lofs in this action, (when it is confidered that we had the entire of the French and rebel army, with nine pieces of cannon, to contend with) was lefs than might have been expected.— One officer and fix rank and file were killed—five officers and twenty-two rank and file were wounded. On the fide of the French, by their own account, above twenty were killed, and about thirty wounded, fourteen of whom were very badly, they were brought in here; of thefe four have fince died in the hofpital. The number of rebels muft have borne a greater proportion, but have not exactly been afcertained.

I have great pleafure in expreffing my entire approbation of the conduct of the officers and foldiers on this occafion. To Lieutenant-colonel Gough, I have to return my warmeft thanks, for the very great zeal and fpirit difplayed by him—

to

to Major Ormsby my thanks are justly due—as also to Captain Waller, of the Limerick regiment, who, with his light company, was extremely active. I have, likewise, to express my obligations to Captain Sleffor, of the Royal Irish artillery, for his conduct in the action, and for his great exertions, under a very heavy fire, to bring off his guns, as well as to Captain Whistler, of the 24th light dragoons, who, with great bravery, met the charge of the French cavalry, and obliged them to retreat.

I have great satisfaction to think, that although we were obliged to retreat, the object of the action was attained—namely, that of saving this town, as, from the acknowledgement of the French officers, it was their intention to have attacked it but for the check they got, and believing that we would not have gone out to meet them, if not supported in our rere; they therefore changed their direction,

*Return of the officers killed and wounded of the Limerick City Regiment, in the above action.*

Colonel Vereker, Lieutenant-Colonel Gough, Major Ormsby, Captain Nash, Ensign Lindon, slightly wounded.—Capt. Crips, wounded through the neck and jaws.—Ensign Rumley, shot through the body, since dead.

Colonel Vereker, previous to his having published the foregoing account, was honoured with a letter from Major-general Nugent, expressing his approbation of his conduct, of which the following is an extract.

Enniskillen, Sept. 9, 1798.

I am extremely happy to find, on enquiry, that although the Limerick City Regiment has suffered much, in the action which they sustained with the French force at Coloonev, the officers are, in general, likely to recover from the wounds they received.

I congratulate you on the gallantry manifested by the whole corps on this occasion, and beg my best compliments may be presented to Lieutenant Colonel Gough, and all the officers.

---

THAT Colonel Vereker is endeared to the loyal inhabitants of Limerick, is evident from the following address.

## TO COLONEL VEREKER.

*By the High-sheriff and Grand Jury of the county of Sligo.—The High-sheriff in the chair.*

RESOLVED, that our warmest thanks are justly due, and are hereby presented to Colonel Vereker, of the Limerick regiment, for his very spirited and judicious conduct, when undiscouraged by their superior numbers and artillery, he marched against the enemy at Colooney, rather than wait their attack; as also for his uncommon exertions and intrepidity during a very severe action, by which the enemy not only received a considerable check, but were diverted from their intended attack and pillage of the town of Sligo, and induced to direct their line of march another way.

Resolved also, that we cannot too fully express our admiration of the officers and privates under Colonel Vereker's command, upon that occasion, for the spirit of perseverance with which they executed all orders under such uncommon disadvantage, and finally accomplished the object of so bold a measure.

JAMES WOOD, High-sheriff.<br>C. O'HARA, Foreman.

OCTOBER 12, 1798.

THE following letter was written by Mr. W. H. G. to a Gentleman in Tyrrell's-pafs, who was pleafed to enclofe it to the Publifher. For former accounts by said correfpondent, fee PART FIRST, pages 70—78, and PART SECOND, pages 120—124. The Editor has ftudied, as far as poffible, to meet the wifhes of thofe Gentlemen who have tranfmitted the materials for this work, by sometimes recapitulating nearly the fame particulars—this being folely his motive, will, he hopes, exculpate him from feeming tautology.

## LETTER XXVIII.

BALLINA, OCTOBER 3, 1798.

*My very dear Friend,*

I WAS in Dublin the evening the exprefs brought intelligence that the French had landed. I went fame day to Naas; it was eleven o'clock at night when I arrived there: you will admit I had a great efcape. The army had marched, I followed, and overtook them in Frankford; we marched from thence to Athlone, where we joined the Commander-in-chief's grand army deftined for Caftlebar; we then marched forward, and encamped at a little village called Balnimore; the next evening we lay at Knock, on the fide of a mountain; from that we proceeded

to

to Tuam, and there encamped; we were then ordered to join General Taylor's brigade, on their march from Sligo. Our regiment (the Armagh) and the Reay fencibles left Tuam camp (confifting of fourteen thoufand brave foldiers), and marched through Caftlerea for Ballaghadareen, where we lay that night; here it was that I met my brother with the light brigade from Blaris—you may conceive what I felt on the occafion. About two in the morning we marched by Swineford for Caftlebar, but the French had given us the flip and went for Sligo; we encamped at Tubbercurry. The French and Limerick militia had a fkirmifh at Colooney;\* many were killed on both fides; we loft two pieces of cannon;—fame evening we lay near Drumahair. Our advanced guard preffed fo hard after the French, that they left feven pieces of cannon, and a great quantity of ammunition, on the road: the road was dreary and wafte, owing to their depredations, the houfes being all plundered. Next day we marched upwards of twenty miles, and encamped near Leitrim. They attempted to break one of the bridges down, but the Heffians charged and killed many of them, which forced them to retire—the road was ftrewed with dead bodies. Near to Cloon they

\* *For this action fee pages* 265—269.

drew

drew up in line of battle, but on our advance they retreated towards Granard. At Ballinamuck they drew up again, and extended their line across a bog, to prevent the cavalry from charging them, and planted their cannon on a hill to the left of the road as it led through the bog: in this order they waited our approach. The light brigade attacked them first; our light company, after a few fires, leaped into their trenches, and dreadful carnage ensued; the French cried for mercy. We ran for four miles before we could get into action; the men forgot all their troubles and fought like furies. We pursued the rebels through the bog—the country was covered for miles round with their slain. We remained for a few days burying the dead—hung General Blake and nine of the Longford militia: we brought an hundred and thirteen prisoners to Carrick-on-Shannon, nineteen of whom we executed in one day, and left the remainder with another regiment to follow our example, and then marched for Boyle, and from that to Cultimagh near Castlebar; some night we received orders to march for Foxford and relieve that place which had been plundered. On our arrival we fortified the town, casting up barriers across the streets—it was well we used this precaution, for we had no cannon, and the rebels next evening surrounded the town in great force, kept up a smart fire for two hours, then gave

gave way; we remained under arms all night. Next day, being Sunday, we brought the Protestant inhabitants with us, and marched for Killala, where we engaged and defeated the rebels with great slaughter, making many prisoners, whom we hung. A few days after the battle we scoured the country towards the mountains, and after a march of thirty miles in one day returned home, leaving many dead.

Our regiment suffered much, being in seventeen engagements. I never suffered so much as on this expedition, from hunger, want of sleep, and fatigue; marching forty-eight hours without tasting meat, nature was almost exhausted.

Yours, &c.<br>W. H. G.

THE following are extracts of a letter which was received by a Gentleman after his liberation at Castlebar, where he had been a prisoner during the time it was in possession of the French— it is given in the words of the writer; and is corroborated by the succeeding accounts.

LETTER

## LETTER XXIX.

KILLISHANDRA, SEPTEMBER, 1798.

*My dear Brother,*

GOD only knows my grief of mind for your present situation—your being yet alive is a strong argument that the hearts of all men are in the hands of the Most High.

Some days before the battle of Ballinamuck we were much alarmed here, although we little thought that the French were so near us. The day previous to the battle our yeomen, horse and foot, Carrickgallon and Oakhill men, one hundred and six in number, went to Ballinamuck, on an information that a vast body of rebels were there the day before; yet after traversing the mountains, not a man could be seen—they returned by Balinalee and Bunlachey. That evening expresses from Ballinamuck informed us that the French were there. The yeomen of that place fled to Ballyconnel and Belturbet. The main body of the French lay in Cloon that night; a Lieutenant West had his horse shot under him, while reconnoitering the enemy—the wounded beast carried his master two miles, when he fell; the helmet was also shot off the Lieutenant's head. The French General and most of the officers agreed to take some rest in Cloon, giving orders that they should not be suffered to sleep but

but two hours—the guard let them sleep four; by which time the English army came much nearer than the French expected. Such is the Providence of God; for had they got seven miles farther in the county Longford, it is said they would have been joined by many thousands, who only waited the coming up of the grand army to lead them. This was the place General Lake's van-guard skirmished with their rear-guard, and from thence to Ballinamuck, four miles from Ballinalee and four miles from Cloon. When the King's army crossed the Shannon, the towns were illuminated for them, and torches held in the streets to give them light. The French being so closely pursued prepared for an unavoidable battle;—they formed on a hill to very great advantage, having a bog on their left, and a bog and lake on their right.

Five flank companies, viz. the Dublin, Armagh, Monaghan, Tipperary, and Kerry, requested General Lake to let them mount behind the Hessians, Carabineers, and Roxburgh, &c. so ardent were they to overtake the enemy. This request was granted, and they soon came up with the foe! The above was our whole force in the action, and no men surely could behave more bravely. Seeing the enemy so advantageously posted, wisdom was needful on the part of our General; a column of our troops faced to the left,

left, and marched behind an eminence, to flank their right wing. Perceiving this, the French retreated to another eminence; to this our artillery marched in front—The enemy had their cannon covered with pikemen, who were about to take our cannon under cover of their own smoke. General Lake aware of their design, ordered the artillery to retreat to another hill, and finding his men so brave, he ordered them to charge the French through the smoke. This they did; and with a terrible war-shout so overwhelmed the French, that they threw up their arms with caps on them, yielding themselves prisoners. Here I should observe that the whole of the French army was not at this time engaged; four hundred and more remained concealed behind the intrenchments, and resolved by treachery to surprise our men, when attacking the rebels: the point was to get them from this hold—a volley or two being fired, our men feigned to retreat. The end was answered; the French rushed out, and our soldiers as suddenly met them;—here the contest was desperate! In a little time the French fell down, offering up their arms, and as our men advanced to receive them, they treacherously arose and fired on our generous unguarded men, and then fell again on their knees: the enraged troops rushed on, and killed numbers of them before they could be prevented. Thus they overpowered,

overpowered, difarmed, and made prifoners, all the French, before the grand army arrived. The rebels expecting no quarters did all poffible harm —fired many cannon-fhot, but to no effect; they fled into a bog, the whole of which was foon furrounded by horfe and foot, who never ceafed while a rebel was alive; after which the Marquis marched off with his prifoners.

There lay dead about five hundred; I went next day with many others to fee them; how awful! to fee that heathy mountain covered with dead bodies, refembling at a diftance flocks of fheep—for numbers were naked and fwelled with the weather. We found fifteen of the Longford militia among the flain. Our lofs was twelve—two of which were Heffians, whom the yeomen took for French and fired on.

The fudden progrefs of fuch a handful of men into the very centre of our ifland, was, I think, a clear comment on the words of Solomon, That "the race is not to the fwift, nor the battle to the ftrong."

Thus, what fix thoufand could not do at Caftlebar, five flank companies and a few cavalry effected at Ballinamuck! Livy fays, in all human affairs, efpecially war, fortune hath a mighty fway; and no where is the event lefs anfwerable to the expectation than in war. Plutarch obferves, there was no temple in Rome dedicated to wifdom or valour, but a moft magnificent one to fortune; fignifying that they afcribed their fuccefs to Providence, not to their courage or conduct. May the loyalifts never lofe fight of this leffon.

---

THAT the *God of Armies* enabled our loyalifts to oppofe the might and power of their determined foes, fhould be individually acknowledged throughout future ages. To their eternal honor, who gratefully avowed this, are the following refolutions recorded in this NARRATIVE.

---

KILLISHANDRA, SEPTEMBER 12, 1798.

AT a PUBLIC VESTRY held this day, it was unanimoufly refolved—

1. That a SOLEMN THANKSGIVING be offered on Sunday next, to

THE LORD GOD OF HOSTS,

for the defeat of *Gallic* invafion and domeftic rebellion, in the heart of the kingdom, at BALLINAMUCK, in the county of Longford, on Saturday laft—and for the fpecial deliverance of this church and town, from the horrors of war and battle.

2. That

2. That our thanks be hereby given to RICHARD IRWIN, of Drumsillah, Esq; for nobly venturing, at the hazard of his life, to reconnoitre the enemy's camp, early on that morning, for communicating important information of their route to the pursuing army, and for kindly relieving the consternation and dismay of this town, by his speedy return, and authentic intelligence.

3. That our thanks be also given to our LOYAL YEOMANRY CORPS, both cavalry and infantry, for their vigilance and strenuous exertions to maintain our inestimable Constitution, and the peace of this district, against foreign and domestic foes, both now and at all times.

4. That these resolutions be recorded in the vestry-book, as a memorial of our gratitude to our DIVINE PROTECTOR and *human defenders* of every description—as a testimony to our CHILDREN, that *WE* have not altogether forgotten

THE GOD OF OUR FATHERS.

(Signed)

WILLIAM HALES, Rector,

RICHARD ANDERSON, } Ch. War.
WILLIAM M'CORMICK, }

*Copy*

*Copy of a letter from Lieut General Lake to Capt Taylor, private Secretary to his Excellency the Lord Lieutenant, dated Camp, near Ballinamuck*

SEPTEMBER 8th, 1798.

Sir,

I have the honour to acquaint you, for the information of his Excellency the Lord Lieutenant, that finding upon my arrival at Ballaghy that the French army had paſſed that place from Caſtlebar, I immediately followed them to watch their motions. Lieut. Col Crawford, who commanded my advanced corps, compoſed of detachments of Hompeſch's and the firſt fencible cavalry, by great vigilance and activity, hung ſo cloſe upon their rear, that they could not eſcape from me, although they drove the country and carried with them all the horſes.

After four days and nights moſt ſevere marching, my column, confiſting of the carabineers, detachments of the 23d light dragoons, the firſt fencible light dragoons, and the Roxburgh fencible dragoons, under the command of Col. Sir Thomas Chapman, Lieut. Col. Maxwell, Earl of Roden, and Captain Kerr; the 3d battalion of light infantry, the Armagh and part of the Kerry millitia, the Reay, Northampton, and Prince of Wales's fencible regiments of infantry, under the command

command of Lieut. Col. Innes, of the 64th regiment, Lord Viscount Gosford, Earl of Glandore, Major Rofs, Lieut. Col. Bulkeley, and Lieut. Col. Macartney, arrived at Cloone about seven this morning, where having received directions to follow the enemy on the same line, whilst his Excellency moved by the lower road to intercept them, I advanced having previously detached the Monaghan light company, mounted behind dragoons to harrafs their rear.

Lieut. Col. Crawford on coming up with the French rear guard, summoned them to surrender; but as they did not attend to his summons he attacked them, upon which upwards of 200 French infantry threw down their arms: under the idea that the reft of the corps would do the same thing—Captain Packenham, Lieut. General of Ordnance, and Major General Cradock rode up to them.—The enemy, however, instantly commenced a fire of cannon and mulketry which wounded General Cradock—upon which I ordered up the third battalion of light infantry, under the command of Lieut. Col. Innes, and commenced the attack upon the enemy's position. The action lasted upwards of half an hour, when the remainder of the column making its appearance, the French surrendered at discretion. The rebels who fled in all directions, suffered severely.

The

The conduct of the cavalry was highly conspicuous. The third light battalion, and part of the Armagh militia (the only infantry that were engaged) behaved most gallantly, and deserve my warmest praise. Lieut. Col. Innes's spirit and judgment contributed much to our success.

To Brig. Gen. Taylor I have to return my most sincere thanks for his great exertions and assistance, particularly on this day—also to Lord Roden, Sir Thomas Chapman, Major Kerr, and Capt. Ferguson, whose example contributed much to animate the troops. I ought not to omit mentioning Lieut. Col. Maxwell, Major Packenham, and Capt. Kerr, whose conduct was equally meritorious—and I feel infinitely thankful to all the commanding officers of corps, who, during so fatiguing a march, encouraged their men to bear it with unremitting perseverance.

To Captain Packenham, Lieut. Col. Clinton (who came to me with orders from Lord Cornwallis) and Major General Cradock, (who joined me in the morning) I am highly indebted for their spirited support; the latter, though early wounded, would not retire from the field during the action.

I acknowledge with gratitude the zeal and activity displayed on all occasions by Lieut. Col. Meade, Major Hardy, Assistant Quarter-Master General, Captains Taylor and Eustace of the engineers,

engineers, Captain Nicholson and my other Aid-de-camp.

I cannot conclude my letter without expressing how much our success is to be attributed to the spirit and activity of Lieut. Col. Crawford. I beg leave to recommend him as a most deserving officer.

I have the honour to be, &c.

G. LAKE.

---

*Return of the killed, wounded, and missing, of the King's forces, at the battle of Ballinamuck, September 8, 1798.*

Lieutenant Stephens, of the Carabineers, wounded. Three privates killed, twelve wounded, and three missing. Eleven horses killed, one wounded, and eight missing.

*Ordnance, Arms, and Ammunition taken.*

Three light French four-pounders.—five ditto, ammunition-waggon, nearly full of made-up ammunition.—One ditto, tumbril.—Seven hundred stand of arms, with belts and pouches.—With a great number of pikes.

*Return of the French Army taken Prisoners at the Battle of Ballinamuck, Sept. 8, 1798.*

General and other officers, - 96
Non-commissioned officers and soldiers, 748
Horses, about - - - 100

Ninety-six rebels taken—three of them called general officers, by the names of Roach, Blake, and Teeling.*

The enemy, in their retreat before the troops under my command, were compelled to abandon nine pieces of cannon, which they had taken in the former actions with his Majesty's forces.

G. LAKE, Lieut. General.

———

THE French marine minister published the following letter from General Humbert to the Executive Directory, the fallacy of which is too notorious to require refutation.

*Lichfield, 2 Vendemiaire, Sept. 25, 1798.*

CITIZENS DIRECTORS,

AFTER having obtained the greatest successes, and made the arms of the French Republic to triumph during my stay in Ireland, I have at

---

* *The two latter since hanged.*

length

length been obliged to submit to a superior force of thirty thousand troops, commanded by Lord Cornwallis.

I am a prisoner of war upon my parole.

(Signed)        HUMBERT.

---

The glorious and decisive event which some time was anticipated at length terminated the rash and idle attempt of our Gallic Enemies and the malignant hopes of our domestic traitors. Our brave and loyal army has taught their foes of every description, that however a temporary advantage may elate their expectations, nothing awaits them in the end but misery and destruction.

The force under General Lake actually engaged with the enemy, did not amount in point of number to the French alone who laid down their arms.

The bravery of all our soldiery was beyond praise; the Armagh militia, in particular, did not fire a single shot, but rushed upon the enemy with fixed bayonets in such a style as to astonish the veterans of the army of Italy.

That gallant Nobleman, Lord Roden, again distinguished himself; his conduct at Clondalken ‡ and Vinegar-hill was even outdone by his bravery at Ballinamuck:—His horse carried him

‡ *The first attack.*

in a rapid charge into the center of the enemy, with eight of his troop; this small but spirited body cut their way back to their own friends through the whole French column.

The number of men lost in this action, compared with the splendid advantages which it has produced, is a wonderful proof of the favor of Providence to the soldiers of religion and loyalty fighting against Atheist regicides.—Surely we may say " *Oh God thy arm was here* ! !"

---

*Copy of the Lord Lieutenant's Letter to the Duke of Portland, relative to the defeat of the French.*

St. Johnstown, Co. of Longford,
9th September, 1798.

*My Lord,*

When I wrote to your Grace on the 5th, I had every reason to believe, from the enemy's movement to Drumahare, that it was their intention to march to the North, and it was natural to suppose, that they might hope that a French force would get into some of the bays in that part of the country, without a succour of which kind every point of direction for their march seemed equally desperate. I received however very early in the morning of the 7th, accounts from General

ral Lake, that they had turned to their right at Drumkerin, and that he had reason to believe that it was their intention to go to Boyle or Carrick on Shannon; in consequence of which, I hastened the march of the troops under my immediate command, in order to arrive before the enemy at Carrick, and directed Major General Moore who was at Tubbercorry, to be prepared in the event of the enemy's movement to Boyle. On my arrival at Carrick I found that the enemy had passed the Shannon at Ballintra, where they had attempted to destroy the bridge, but General Lake followed them so closely, that they were not able to effect it. Under these circumstances, I felt pretty confident, that one more march would bring this disagreeable warfare to a conclusion; and having obtained satisfactory information that the enemy had halted for that night at Cloone, I marched, with the troops at Carrick, at ten o'clock, on the night of the 7th, to Mohill, and directed Gen. Lake to proceed at the same time to Cloone, which is about three miles from Mohill, by which movement I should be able to join with General Lake in the attack of the enemy, if they should remain at Cloone, or to intercept their retreat, if they should as it was most probable, retire on the approach of our army. On my arrival at Mohill, soon after day-break, I found that the enemy had begun to move towards

wards Granard; I therefore proceeded, with all possible expedition, to this place, through which I was assured, on account of a broken bridge, that the enemy must pass in their way to Granard, and directed Gen. Lake to attack the enemy's rear, and impede their march as much as possible, without bringing the whole of his corps into action. Lieut. Gen. Lake performed this service with his usual attention and ability, and the † enclosed letter, which I have just received from him, will explain the circumstances which produced an immediate surrender of the enemy's army. The copy ‡ of my orders which I enclose will show how much reason I have to be satisfied with the exertions of the troops, and I request that your Grace will be pleased to inform his Majesty, that I have received the greatest assistance from the General and Staff who have served with the army.

I have, &c.

(Signed)           CORNWALLIS.

*His Grace*

*The Duke of Portland, &c.*

† *See Pages* 280—4
‡ *See Page* 289

**GENERAL**

## GENERAL ORDERS.

*Head Quarters, near St. John's Town,*

*9th September,* 1798.

Lord Cornwallis cannot too much applaud the zeal and spirit which has been manifested by the army, from the commencement of the operations against the invading enemy, until the surrender of the French forces.

The perseverance with which the Soldiers supported the extraordinary marches which were necessary to stop the progress of the very active enemy, does them the greatest credit; and Lord Cornwallis heartily congratulates them on the happy issue of their meritorious exertions.

The corps of yeomenry, in the whole country through which the army has passed, have rendered the greatest services, and are peculiarly entitled to the acknowledgments of the Lord Lieutenant, for their not having tarnished that courage and loyalty which they displayed in the cause of their King and Country, by any acts of wanton cruelty towards their deluded fellow subjects.

## TO THE READER.

WHEN the FIRST PART of this Work was put to Prefs, it was the intention of the Editor to have introduced *original letters* only, but from the counfel of feveral literary Gentlemen he has been convinced of the neceffity of receding from fuch previous determination—he therefore inferts the following letter, which he hopes will juftify this deviation.

## LETTER XXX.

DUBLIN, OCTOBER 23, 1799.

*Anniverfary of the Irifh Rebellion,* 1641.

Sir,

I HAVE looked over your *proof fheets*, and beg you will accept my thanks for the fatisfaction they have afforded. The SECOND PART of your Narrative contains a great variety of interefting matter. I fincerely hope your laudable exertions may be crowned with fuccefs. You lament that fome inaccuracies have gone through part of the *impreffion*—I fuppofe you mean *literal errors:* indeed, my friend, when I confider the innumerable difadvantages under which your undertaking has laboured—from the variety of illegible manufcripts, manuscripts, your absence from home, &c. it is matter of astonishment to me that it is so correct: with the last line of your favour I most heartily agree, that the whole will have this recommendation, "AUTHENTICITY."

Permit me now to humbly submit for your consideration, to annex (by way of appendix or otherwise) the enclosed. I know it is your intention to publish the whole at some future day, as an history, introducing the different anecdotes, &c. you mention; but, my friend, give me leave to tell you, that hundreds will purchase the present who may never behold your future Publication, to whom the following, which I have carefully abridged, may be very acceptable.

Yours, truly.

## APPENDIX.

*An authentic Extract from the Information of Mr. Grandy, at Duncannon-fort.*

County of Wexford, } RICHARD GRANDY to wit. } of Ballystraco, in the county of Wexford, farmer, came this day before us his Majesty's justices of the peace for said county, and maketh oath on the Holy Evangelists that he was attacked and seized at the cross roads of Kilbride in said county on Sunday the third of June instant, between the hours of nine and ten o'clock in the morning, by several persons armed with guns, pikes and spears; by many persons whose names this deponent knows not, though their faces were very familiar to him; that examinant was conducted to the rebel camp at Carrick-Byrne in said county; was brought to Mr. King's house at Scollobogue in said county; that he was introduced into a room where he saw Bagnel Harvey of Bargy-Castle in said county, esquire, with a few more whom deponent did not know; the deponent was closely examined by the said Bagnel Harvey as to the state of Ross and Duncannon Fort, and whether he was an Orange-man or an United man; that said Bagnel Harvey proffered him to take the oath of an United Irishman, and become one of their community; that at last deponent obtained a pass from said Bagnel Harvey, with which he came as far as Bryanstown, where he was stopped by the guard of rebels who brought him prisoner to Scollobogue-House, where he was confined till the Tuesday morning following, with many other Protestants; that about nine o'clock John Murphy of Loughnageer in said county who had the command of the Rosegarland rebel corps, and was the officer of the guard over the prisoners, had ordered them out by fours to be shot by his company of rebels, till thirty-five were massacred; that the rebel

spear-men

spear-men used to take pleasure in piercing the victims through with spears, and in exultation lick their bloody spears; that while this horrid scene was acting the barn at said Scollobogue, in which were above one hundred Protestants (as deponent heard and believes) was set on fire and all consumed to ashes; that examinant's life was spared because said Murphy knew said Bagnel Harvey had given him a pass, and through his intercession with said Murphy, Loftus Frizzell was likewise spared; sayeth they were both tyed and conveyed within a mile of Ross where they met said Bagnel Harvey, Cornelious Grogan, of Johnstown in said county, Esq. said William Devereux, and many others unknown to deponent, retreating from the battle of Ross; also sayeth that said Bagnel Harvey ordered said Murphy to take the prisoners to his lodgings at Collop's Well, where he gave a pass to Loftus Frizzell, but refused to give one to deponent, lest he should go to Duncannon Fort, and report what deponent had heard and seen; faith that he heard and believes it to be a fact that said Cornelious Grogan had the command of the Barony of Fort rebel troops at the battle of Ross; faith that he was taken to Foulke's-mill in said county that night, where he continued for two days under a guard dressing the wounded; that he was afterwards conveyed to Ballymitty in said county,

when

when he obtained a pass from Edward Murphy parish priest of said place, to pass and re-pass through his district for the purpose of curing the wounded; saith that he was sent to Taghmon where the sitting rebel magistrates John Brien, James Harpar, Joseph Cullamore, and Matthew Commons were of opinion that deponent might with the priest's pass have gone back again and remain there; sayeth that he strolled along the sea side under the protection of this pass till at last he effected his escape across the ferry of Bannow to Feathard on Friday evening the 22d instant, and from thence to Duncannon Fort this morning; deponent further sayeth that he attended mass celebrated by Edward Murphy, parish priest of Bannow; that after mass he heard said Edward Murphy preach a sermon, in which he said " Brethren you see you are victorious every " where, that the balls of the Hereticks fly about " you without hurting you, that few of you have " fallen whilst thousands of the Hereticks are " dead, and the few that have fallen was from " deviating from our cause and the want of faith; " that this visibly is the work of God, who now " is determined, that the Hereticks who have " reigned upwards of one hundred years, should " be now extirpated, and the true Catholic reli- " gion established;" and deponent sayeth this sermon was preached after the battle of Ross, and

sayeth

fayeth he has heard several sermons preached by the priests to the same effect; and further sayeth that he has heard several of the rebels who had been at the battle of Enniscorthy and elsewhere declare, that Edward Roche the priest did constantly catch the bullets that came from his Majesty's army in his hand and give them to the rebels to load their guns with; deponent further sayeth that any Protestant who was admitted into the rebel army was first baptized by the Roman Catholic priest, and that every Protestant who refused to be baptized was put to death, and that many to save their lives suffered themselves to be baptized.

*Sworn before his Majesty's justices of the peace for said county this 23d day of June 1798, at Duncannon Fort.*

Bound in the sum of two hundred pounds to prosecute, when called on, this examination with effect.

GEORGE OGLE.
ISAAC CORNOCK.
JOHN HENRY LYSTER.
JOHN KENEDY.

RICHARD GRANDY.

( A true Extract. )

## SUBSTANCE OF A TRIAL AT WEXFORD,
### Summer Assizes, 1799.

PHELIM FARDY was indicted and tried before Baron Smith, for the murder of a person unknown, at Scolabogue, on the fifth of June, 1798.

First witness for the crown.—Richard Silvester proved, that on the fourth of June, 1798, the rebels assembled at Scolabogue, to a very great number, armed with guns, pikes, and a variety of other weapons; that about two o'clock in the afternoon, on the same day, they marched to Corbit-hill, near the town of New-Ross: that a party under the command of a Captain Murphy, of Loughnageer, consisting of about three hundred men, were left on guard over the prisoners at Scolabogue: that on the morning of the fifth of June, the day following, between the hours of five and six o'clock, an express came to Capt. Murphy to destroy the prisoners, for that the army were getting the better at Ross; Captain Murphy replied he would not without a written order from the General: that shortly after another express arrived, with the same orders to destroy the prisoners, saying, that the King's army were cutting them off; that they would be immediately there and liberate the prisoners, and
that

that they would be ten times more outrageous if they were releafed; Captain Murphy refufed, as before, to obey thefe orders: that fhortly after a third exprefs arrived, faying, that the prieft gave orders to deftroy the prifoners. Upon this authority being mentioned the rebels became outrageous, fome of them pulled off their clothes with zeal to begin the bloody deed: that witnefs on feeing the prifoners in the dwelling-houfe pulling out for execution, turned afide, when he was met by a rebel who knew him, who advifed witnefs to come with him, in order to avoid the horrors going on: that on witnefs going away, another rebel ftruck witnefs on the back with a pike, and with fury in his looks ordered witnefs to follow him, faying, he would let his guts out if he difobeyed: that witnefs followed this rebel to the barn, where a number of men, women, and children were confined; and faw the rebels with violence endeavouring to fet the barn on fire: that the prifoners fhrieking and crying out for mercy, crouded to the back door of the barn, which they pulled open, and at times pulled the door between them and the rebels, till their fingers and hands were cut off, and until they were overpowered by a conftant fupply of bundles of ftraw on fire flung in upon them, while others were piking and fhooting them: that witnefs faw a child, who had been fhattered by

the

the door, when it fell acrofs the frame, force itfelf almoft out of the barn, when a rebel on perceiving the child inftantly darted his pike into it, when it gave a fhriek and expired! By this time the cries and moans of the prifoners died away: that during the time witnefs was at the barn, he heard a conftant fire kept up at the dwelling-houfe; that on his return to the dwelling-houfe he faw a number of dead bodies before the hall-door, fome of which he knew; that he faw one man among the dead on his knees, while the rebel women and men were ftripping and rifling the bodies of the dead; that he was near the prifoner, Phelim Fardy, who had a mufket in his hand; that he heard Fardy call out to them who were rifling the dead, to quit the range of his fhot; that inftantly witnefs faw Fardy prefent his mufquet at the man on his knees; that witnefs turned about, and on hearing the report of the fhot, looked back and faw the man expiring.

*Queftion from the jury.*—Are you certain that the prifoner is the man you faw that day prefent the mufquet at the man on his knees?—Anf. I am; for I have known him thefe twelve years paft, I could not be miftaken.

Mr. Richard Grandy,* fecond witnefs for the crown, depofed, that witnefs was a prifoner, with many

* *See his affidavit pages* 291—295.

many others, on the fifth of June, 1798, in the dwelling-house at Scolabogue; that an order being given to put the prisoners to death, witness went on his knees, and on several of his fellow-prisoners being brought out for execution, he, the witness, went to a window, in hopes he might see some person he knew, in expectation of being saved; that he saw the prisoner, Phelim Fardy, near the window, at the front of the house, with a musquet in his hand, and his hands and face blackened with powder; that immediately two men seized witness, and brought him out for execution, where he saw two men on their knees to be shot; that a rebel snapped his musquet twice at one of them, that he then struck his flint with his knife, and presented a third time, when he shot him; that immediately after Captain Murphy came up to witness, and called him by name, and said he should not be put to death, and put him back into the room where he came from; that there he saw a man on his knees, who aftewards he found to be a Mr. Frizell; that he came over and intreated witness to intercede for him; that immediately after Captain Murphy called out to know if all the prisoners were executed, and came into the room, and on seeing Mr. Frizell he ordered him for execution, when Grandy on his knees begged for his life, that he was a stranger from Dublin;

Captain

Captain Murphy, enraged at the requeſt, ſaid he had a mind to bring out Grandy for daring to intercede, and have him executed with Mr. Frizell; that inſtantly after two rebel females came in, and intreated Captain Murphy not to put the young man to death, as it would be a great pity; by which means Mr. Frizell's life was ſpared.

Proſecution cloſed.—The priſoner did not produce any witneſs.

The jury retired for a moment, and brought in their verdict guilty. Inſtantly the judge pronounced ſentence of death in a very awful manner, and regretted he could not order him for immediate execution, as the heinouſneſs of his crimes, ſo clearly and fully proved, made him a fit object for public example.

On a trial at the court-martial about a week before the aſſizes, it was proved that a man of the name of Miſkella was tried, found guilty, and hanged for murders at Scollabogue, who was for his ſuperlative atrocities at Scollabogue, called the *true Roman*, for he would not wince at putting to death *Heretics!*

## A FEW AUTHENTIC ATROCITIES.

VERIDICUS† (a publication which has passed through several editions, without any attempting a refutation) selects the following from a catalogue of dreadful atrocities.

"DURING the rebel encampment on Vinegar-hill, they daily led out of the different prisons; from twenty to thirty Protestants, whom, after a mock trial, they butchered in presence of, and as a regale to, the rebels while on parade.

"Some scenes of the deepest tragic woe occurred in the course of these butcheries; and it is universally believed, that not less than four hundred Protestants were murdered in this manner on that hill. Many of them were magistrates, men of fortune, opulent farmers, or shopkeepers, whose wealth might have tempted their avarice, or provoked their envy; but the poorest Protestants were equally the objects of their sanguinary fury.

"One or two instances shew how these scenes of savagery were conducted. John Connors, his wife and daughter, were taken prisoners to the hill, where they saw John Plunket and J. Rigley, two Protestants, on their knees, in front of the rebels on parade, who formed a half moon. While these three prisoners were on their knees, one

† *Published by Milliken, Grafton-street.*

James D'Arcy, an opulent corn-factor, stepped forward, and shot Rigley with a horse-pistol; he then charged it with great deliberation, and told Plunket, insultingly, that he would do his business, and then shot him. Having charged it again, he shot Connors, and he, on falling, dragged his old wife with him, as she had put her arm under his to support him. His poor old wife told D'Arcy, that she now wished he would kill her; on which he swore he would do so, and was proceeding to effect it, but some rebels more humane than the rest, interposed, and prevented him. These circumstances were related on oath at Wexford, by the widow and daughter of Connors, on the trial of D'Arcy. Brien Neal, of Ballybrennan, was led to execution in presence of his aged father and a brother. Having asked for a fair trial, he was refused. He then made a request, that instead of torturing him with pikes, they would shoot him; on which a rebel struck him on the head with a carpenter's adze, after which he staggered a few steps, and fell; when one Joseph Murphy shot him. His father was then put on his knees, but the executioner missed fire three times at him; on this, Father Roach, the General, who presided at the execution, desired him to try whether the firelock would go off in the air; and having accordingly made the experiment, it went off. Father Roach, thereupon,

upon, declared him innocent, and discharged him with a protection, having imputed his escape to the interposition of Divine Providence.

Unheard of tortures were practised on the hill. A Protestant saved by the interposition of a rebel captain, who had a warm friendship for him, swore the following affidavit before a Magistrate; " That on the 1st of June, he saw a man sitting on the ground there, with no other clothes to cover him than a piece of ragged blanket: that his eyes were out, his head and body were swelled, and his cheeks were covered with ulcers: that on deponent's exclaiming what a miserable object that was! the poor wretch uttered some inarticulate sounds, but could not speak, from which he supposed that his tongue had been cut out. That an armed rebel, whom he believed to be one of the guards, said, that he was under punishment, and mentioned something of slow death, indicating as he supposed, that he was to suffer such a death."

Many Protestants were massacred in their camp at Carrickbyrne, with the same circumstances of cruelty and barbarity, as took place at Vinegar-hill; and similar atrocities were practised at the camp near Gorey, which continued in the vicinity of that town for many days.

*Authentic*

*Authentic Account of the Behaviour and Confeſſion of James Beaghan, who was executed on Vinegar-hill, on the 24th of Auguſt, 1799.*

THE day but one before Beaghan's execution, he requeſted that Captain Boyd might be ſent for, to whom he made the following confeſſion:

I JAMES BEAGHAN, acknowledge and confeſs that I am guilty of the crime for which I am to ſuffer, but that I did not commit it from ill-will to the people that were murdered, but from the order of Luke Byrne; ‡ I could not diſobey him—no perſon dare refuſe to obey the orders of the commanders. I am ſure that any perſon in command could ſave the lives of the poor; every man that was a Proteſtant was called an Orangeman, and every one was to be killed, from the pooreſt man in the country. Before the rebellion, I never heard there was any hatred between Roman-catholics and Proteſtants, they always lived peaceably together. I always found the Proteſtants better maſters and more indulgent landlords than my own religion; during the rebellion, I never ſaw any one interfere to prevent murder, but one Byrne, who ſaved a man. I think all that were preſent were as guilty as thoſe that perpetrated the murders. It was thinking that we were all equally guilty that prevented me

‡ *A commander of the rebels.*

from

from flying the country. The women were numerous, and were as bad as the men. The rebels treated the prisoners with great severity, very different from the way that I have been used in goal. They thought it no more a sin to kill a Protestant than a dog; had it not been that they were so soon quashed, they would have fought with each other for the property of the Protestants. They were beginning before the battle of Vinegar-hill. Ever since the rebellion, I never heard one of the rebels express the least sorrow for what was done; on the contrary, I have heard them say, they were sorry that whilst they had the power they did not kill more, and that there were not half enough killed. I know that the rebels were determined to rise if the French should come; and I believe they did not give up half their arms. There are guns, bayonets, and pikes hid in the country.

‖ Now, Gentlemen, remember what I tell you, if you and the Protestants are ever in the power of the Catholics again, as they are now in yours, they will not leave one of you alive; you will all go smack smooth—even them that campaigned

‖ *From this mark Beaghan spoke without having been asked any questions, and spoke with an earnestness and in a manner that shewed his sincerity.*

with them, if things had gone well with them, would in the end have been killed. I have heard them say so many times.

  Taken before us, August 23, 1799.

    CHRISTIAN WILSON, Sheriff.
    J. H. LYSTER, Justice P.

    his
JAMES ✕ BEAGHAN,
   mark.      (A Copy.)

  Having arrived at the place of execution, Captain Boyd brought him aside, and read his confession, and asked him if it was correctly taken down, to which he answered in the affirmative. Just as the executioner was about to turn him off, he called out, saying "Stop," and lifting up his cap, said with a very loud voice, "Captain Boyd, you have taken down my confession perfectly correct; if it was not for the Priests I never would have been guilty of murder, nor have dragged five unfortunate persons out of the windmill to be murdered; amongst these five were the son of old Minchin the carpenter."

HOW very depraved muſt the rebel horde have been, will appear, when on ſome occaſions neither old age nor unoffending youth ſcarcely eſcaped the effects of their bigotry and revenge. On a recent trial\* (the *ſubject* of which ſome ſtrangely attempt to juſtify) dreadful inſtances of this have appeared—among ſeveral, is that of

JOSHUA CHASE, a feeble old man, in the eightieth year of his age, who was taken priſoner in Tinehaly, the ſixteenth of June, carried to the camp at Mount-Pleaſant, and guarded with ſeveral other loyaliſt priſoners, by a large party of pikemen, amongſt whom was one Mergin, ſerjeant of the guard. On the ſeventeenth Mergin charged Chaſe with being an Orangeman, and a maker of Orangemen, and having three ſons Orangemen, which he denied. Mergin deſired Chaſe to bleſs himſelf; he could not, except by ſaying the Lord bleſs him. Then have you any religion? Chaſe ſaid he had, and that his religion was derived from the Scriptures. No, ſaid Mergin, your religion is derived from a rogue and a whore, and groſsly abuſed him, and ſaid Henry VIII. and Queen Elizabeth, were the rogue and

\* *Publiſhed by M‘Kenzie, College-green.*

whore;

whore; upon which Chafe replied, he had read the Scriptures, from Genefis to Revelations, and had not feen the name of King Henry VIII. or Queen Elizabeth. Mergin then tied Chafe's arms, which he drew backwards by a cord, until they were near drawn out of the fockets, whereby he fuffered great pain; he was tied by Mergin about the hour of eleven, and continued in that fituation until about four or five in the evening; fome time after his being fo tied he was ordered by Mergin to go on his knees, and then a party of gun-men were called for to fhoot him, while others called out to pike him.

William Byrne coming up, Mergin faid to him, Captain, what fhall we do with them? meaning Berry and Chafe, who were lying on the ground tied, which Berry was afterwards in the evening fhot.—Mr. *William Byrne*, of *Ballymanus*, anfwered, I don't care what the devil you do with them, " if you don't chufe to kill them put them in the guard-houfe."

Mergin took Chafe twice before a perfon who affumed the character of juftice of the peace, and charged him as being a maker of Orangemen; Chafe defired the juftice to put Mergin to his oath, which the juftice declined, faying it was fabbath-day, and he would not adminifter an oath. Mergin afterwards brought Chafe back to the guard, and said he would not trouble himself to look for witnesses, to prove him being an Orangeman, but would make the matter short; he then made Chase lie down, when he swore he would cut his head off, and laid the edge of a sword across his neck, which he repeated a second time. Two gentlemen, in some short time after, came riding by, who Chase understood were principal commanders, one of them said to him, old man, come here, what fault have you committed? Chase said he could not tell, and requested he would call any honest man in the camp to tell what he had done; the gentlemen then called aloud, and desired to know what Chase had done, and having again called to the same effect, and no one appearing, said person, who Chase believes was General *Perry*, ordered him to be set at liberty, and sent a man to guard him out of the camp. When William Byrne, and the rebel party, which consisted principally of horse, came into Tinehaly, they ordered that such of the inhabitants as were Roman-catholics, should put up lights in their houses, none of which were burned, but all others were.

---

WILLIAM GRAHAM about the age of fourteen, was taken by the rebels and brought to Mount Pleasant, he and other prisoners were guarded

guarded by pikemen, and Mergin was the ferjeant. William Byrne came into the ring, with a drawn fword in his hand, and was afked by fome of them what fhould be done with the *children?* Byrne anfwered, " damn them, kill them or do what you like with them."

SINCE the foregoing part of this Work has been committed to prefs, fome Gentlemen have called upon the Editor, and requefted that the fubfequent accounts might be added, which are printed agreeably to their manufcripts, and given as

## SUPPLEMENTARY.

### LETTER XXXI.

TINEHALY, OCTOBER 25, 1799.

Sir,

ON Whitfun-Sunday eve, 1798, Lieutenant Bockey, of the Camolin yeomen-cavalry, being on piquet between his own houfe and Camolin, was furrounded and inhumanly murdered by a party of rebels, who brought him to his own houfe, which they burned; they alfo killed and wounded fome of his party. At break of day the next morning, a party of the yeomenry and true blues of Tinahely, on piquet near Wicklow-gap,

gap, perceiving the house of (Smith) a yeoman, at Anagh, on fire, made towards it, and observing some people on the rocks of Conna-hill, they pursued them, and took five, one a well-dressed clever young man (son to Laughlin Finn, of Camolin, in the county of Wexford, a respectable farmer), upon whose clothes was discovered blood; they were then brought to the guard-house of Tinehaly, where an express arrived with the account of Mr. Bookey's murder; and as, upon examination, they could give no proper account of themselves, they were ordered back to Wicklow-gap, there to be shot and buried. It has since been more fully proved that they murdered Lieutenant Bookey. The same morning another party of the yeomenry and true blues of Tinehaly, took one Doyle, at Kilpipe church-yard; it appeared that he had been a tenant to Mr. Bookey of Doneshall, brother to the deceased Lieutenant; he rode one horse and led another, and was after conveying a son of his to the county of Wicklow mountains, who had been concerned in the murder of Mr. Bookey— he was brought to Carnew, where he suffered death. Another party from Tinehaly, at Ballinglin, took three men with pikes, who were afterwards shot near the church of Kilcommon. Wicklow-gap, and that part of the country, being the pass from the counties of Kildare and

Wicklow

Wicklow to Wexford, there was not a night after until the seventeenth of June, that the same loyal people, and the yeomenry and loyalists of Shillelagh and that neighbourhood, by scouring the country, did not meet with more or less armed rebels (but not in great force) going back and forward, whom they dispatched,—not many of the loyalists lost their lives. A Mr. Mathias Dowse, and a lodger of his, were killed by a party of rebels the night before Colonel Walpole was defeated.‡ On account of the defeat of Colonel Walpole, and the rebels being in possession of Gorey, &c. General Loftus retreated with his army, and gave directions that all the Shillelah yeomenry and loyalists should evacuate that country, and march to some garrison town; upon which they all went to Hacket's-town. On the sixteenth of June, at night, twenty thousand rebels marched from Limerick camp near Gorey, to Mount Pleasant, near Tinehaly, intending to burn Tinehaly on the seventeenth (which they did), and on that night to march to and attack Hacket's-town, which they were well informed had but about four hundred yeomenry, and thirty of the Antrim militia for its protection; providentially, at twelve o'clock that day, General Dundas, with a large army and train of artillery,

‡ *For this action see pages* 121—4.

marched

marched in. Tinehaly being in view, and on fire, application was made to the General to relieve it; he declined going himself, but gave the yeomenry permission; upon which, the Shillelah infantry, Hacket's-town infantry, and one hundred and fifty of the True Blues, with Lord Roden's, Captain Hume's, the Shillelah and Ballaghkeen troops of cavalry, volunteered, and marched under the command of Lord Roden. The rebels had piquets on the different hills round the town, and on the approach of the corps before-mentioned they precipitately retreated to Mount-Pleasant; on the infantry entering Tinehaly (by which some of the houses were saved), the rebels fired their cannon, but, providentially, there were no lives lost. Lieutenant Braddell, on Tinehaly-hill, narrowly escaped one of their balls, and on Captain Wainright's troop crossing the bridge of Tinehaly, two cannon balls lodged in the arch thereof. Lord Roden and Captain Hume's troop met with the rebel piquet that had been on Rofsbawn-hill, and killed twenty-eight of them. On their passing through the church-lane to Tinehaly, branches of the trees were lopped off over their heads, by the rebel cannon, yet not one of the party were killed. This has been accounted for since—those who pointed the cannon being the artillery-men belonging to Colonel Walpole, who were taken prisoners, and were determined to preserve the loyalists. The rebels, that night, instead of attacking Hacket's-town, quit Mount-Pleasant, and encamped at Kilcavan,† where they were attacked next day, by General Dundas, and that night retreated towards Vinegar-hill. The yeomenry and loyalists on their return home, after the defeat of the rebels at Vinegar-hill,‡ killed many of them who were found hiding, particularly Capt. Doyle, of Knockbranden, by a Tinehaly True Blue.

A reconnoitering party, of about fifty men, went to Tineban, where they met with a number of cars laden with property, supposed to be taken from Enniscorthy, escorted by at least one hundred and fifty rebels, men and women, whom they defeated, killing upwards of fifty. They proceeded to take the cars to Tinehaly, but perceiving upwards of five hundred horsemen, on the road from Gorey (where they had murdered every Protestant they could meet), pursuing them, the party was obliged, after taking the horses, to leave the cars behind. In this attack a rebel

---

† *For this action see pages* 233—239.
‡ *For this defeat see* PART *the* FIRST, *pages* 75—78.

leader

leader was killed, having one of the Castletown cavalry helmets on him, which, with a cockade, and the horses, were brought into Tinehaly.

After the defeat of the rebels at Vinegarhill, the loyalists whose houses were saved, went home; about one o'clock in the morning of the thirtieth of June, a Gentleman living on an eminence near Tinehaly, on seeing the reflection of fire, went to the window of his room, from whence he saw several houses in the neighbourhood in a blaze, particularly on the way from Ridenagh rebel camp towards Mr. Brownrigg's of Wingfield, whose house they also set on fire. A rebel party went to burn the house of Mr. Thomas Dowse, but a reconnoitering party from the Tinehaly corps firing upon them, obliged them to fly. By this time the great body of the rebels were going over Wicklow-gap, making for Carnew; an express was immediately sent there, with this account, and another to Gorey, which occasioned a party of the Ancient Britons, Gorey and Wingfield yeomenry corps, to march for the relief of Carnew; but unfortunately the rebels being so numerous, and from a disadvantage in the situation of the place, these last corps were nearly surrounded in the road at Ballyellis, and several, particularly the Ancient Britons, were killed; the women had stopped the only two paſſages by which the King's troops could eſcape, with timber, cars, kiſhes, &c. ſo that had it not been for an excellent manœuvre of about thirty of the yeomen-cavalry, who, (not being in uniform) leaving their horſes, took poſſeſſion of a dry pond, and entrenched themſelves; the rebels ſuppoſed them to be their friends, ſurrounding theſe loyal people, whereby they might have put all of them to death; but theſe brave fellows fired from their intrenchments, killed ſeveral, and put the remainder in ſuch confuſion, as gave ſuch of the corps as had eſcaped an opportunity of making their way through the interrupted paſſages.

The rebels who were encamped at Ballymanus, and thoſe at Camolin, met at Monaſeed, where, upon holding a council of war, and being informed there were no troops in Carnew, but the yeomenry of the town, they determined to kill every Proteſtant, man, woman and child, therein, and deſtroy the town. An expreſs being ſent off to Tomacork, where the Coollattin corps, under Capt. Chamney, and the Tinehaly corps, under Capt. Moreton, were: they immediately marched to Carnew, and entered it at *one* end; juſt as the rebels were ſetting fire to the few remaining houſes at the *other*, and Mr. Blayney's extenſive diſtillery.

distillery. These corps gave three cheers, and advanced up the street, while the Carnew corps, under Capt. Swan, commenced a heavy fire from the large malt-house they had occupied. This unexpected reception, after the horrid business they had been engaged in, threw the rebels into confusion, and they retreated into the county of Wexford, followed for a short distance by the yeomenry.

Next day the corps marched off to Ballyellis, and brought in the dead bodies of the loyalists, which were either interred in Carnew church-yard, or delivered to their friends. There were some very worthy and respectable people lost on that day.

On the morning of the second of July, two days after, the rebels, in great numbers, appeared in view of the town, but made no attempt on it; they marched off towards Tullow, piking every Protestant they met with, particularly Messrs. G. Driver, the celebrated boot-maker of Tinehaly, William Waters of Ballykelly, and James Tuamley, all inoffensive harmless men; but being pursued by the Shillelah yeomenry corps, and joined on the road by the Wingfield cavalry, they wheeled about at Mullinacuff, and turned towards Tinehaly, until they came on Ballyrahine-hill.

## BATTLE OF BALLYRAHINE-HILL.

Here these yeomenry corps attacked them, and killed several; they were actually on the retreat, when one of the corps having nearly exhausted their ammunition, gave way, which encouraged them so much, that they all poured down, and compelled the yeomenry corps to retreat. Capt. Moreton of the Tinehaly corps, and Lieutenant Chamney of the Coollattin corps, with about fifty men, retreated into Ballyrahine-house, on which the rebels commenced an attack, and kept it up until three o'clock next morning. They then encamped on Fort-town-hill, and burned the house there; they also set fire to Ballyrahine haggard and out-offices, and during the night were constantly endeavouring to set fire to the house. Several fellows in the act of doing so, advanced to the very hall-door, with furze, pitch, and straw, *all* covered with feather-beds; the son of a confidential servant of Captain Chamney's, was killed in the act of setting fire to the stables. It is now known, that at least one hundred and thirty were killed, besides many wounded, from Ballyrahine-house that night; having the advantage of the light from the burning of Fort-town-house on one side, and of the haggard on the other. They retreated early next morning (continuing their burning and killing) to Ballymanus.

The

The celebrated Bridget Dolan,* giving information on oath against murderers, lately told a circumstance worthy of notice, which happened that night. Several wounded rebels were taken into a cabin near Ballyrahine-house, to be dressed; *Biddy* was very active and handy at that business; her story was, that one man had come to that cabin for a coal of fire, and desired that several there might go with him, to see the *heretics* in Ballyrahine-house made ashes of. Several went with him, but in a short time the same man returned: when she asked him what brought him back so soon, he said he was wounded; upon which she desired him to sit down, until the other wounded men were dressed; when preparing to dress him, to her very great surprise, she found him dead, having expired without a groan or sigh. There was a rebel chief killed (supposed to be a priest), who was carried to a cabin at New-town, where he lingered for some hours, and early in the morning, before they left Forttown-hill, a party buried him at Mullinacuff church-yard; from whence he was very lately taken, put into a coffin, and brought to the upper part of the county of Wexford. Had it not been for the deaths of the two worthy and much regretted Captains Chamney and Nickson, a son

---

* *See Byrne's Trial.*

of Lieutenant Chamney, and a few other respectable loyalists, who fell upon this occasion, this battle would have been as glorious and as well worthy of notice in your publication probably, as any other that happened. The different acts of courage, &c. of these loyal people, and the kindness of Providence in their escape, has been very signal, not one in the house was injured.

LETTER XXXII.

CARNEW, OCTOBER 30, 1799.

Sir,

An account of the murder of Lieut. Bookey, having reached the Shilelagh corps on Whitsun-Sunday, the Shillelagh cavalry under Captain Wainright, the Coolatin and Carnew companies under Captains Chamney and Swan, and about fifty Antrim militia under Captain I. Rowan, making about forty cavalry and one hundred and fifty infantry, paraded in Carnew about 12 o'clock, and immediately marched in pursuit of the rebels—after picking up a few stragglers in arms, they got information about 3 o'clock, that the rebels were in great force on a hill called Killthomas, between Camolin and Carnew, where our small party immediately proceeded, and found them drawn up on the summit of the hill, with a high ditch in front, and their officers mounted and

and riding along their lines. On our appearing on the road under them, they gave a savage yell and beckoned with their hats, daring us to the combat—they seemed to be about three thousand and great numbers of women were among them.

## BATTLE OF KILLTHOMAS.

Our small party were ordered to advance up the hill by companies, and form as they came up behind a ditch about 150 yards in front of the rebels, which was done with great steadiness, neither party firing a shot—each continued some time in their position, until at last the rebels came over the ditch and fired at us, which was returned briskly, and after two or three rounds our gallant little party leaped over the ditch in their front and immediately advanced up the hill: the rebels instantly broke and dispersed in all directions, leaving coats, shoes, arms of all descriptions, and several handkerchiefs of provisions behind.—The cavalry pursued them until night, and killed great numbers. We all returned to Carnew about 8 o'clock without any loss on our side, except Captain Rowan's mare which was killed—Mr. Cope rector of Carnew, and several of the loyal inhabitants partook of the fatigues of the day.

## ATTACK UPON LEIXLIP.

IN the night of the twenty-sixth of May, 1798, a large body of rebels approached the town of Leixlip, which, from its contiguity to the metropolis, seemed to be an object of importance to them; as there was no barrack there, and only a few military stationed in the place, the rebels advanced with much confidence under the direction of one *Smith*, their leader. Very fortunately Colonel GORDON had arrived in the course of the evening, with a detachment of the Inverness fencibles and two field-pieces. As the rebels came near the town, they perceived the two pieces of cannon, but still supposing there was only a trifling guard, they became elated with the idea of seizing and carrying off the cannon.

With this expectation they rushed furiously forward, when a fire of grape-shot was opened upon them; their progress was instantly checked, and they were thrown into some confusion. Col. GORDON, taking advantage of this circumstance, ordered a charge with fixed bayonets, which threw the enemy into such consternation, that they fled in all directions, leaving behind them between fifty and sixty in killed and wounded.

This loss was felt so severely, and the rebels were impressed with such an opinion of the steadiness

diness and courage of the *Inverness* regiment, that Leixlip remained afterwards free from any attack during the existence of the rebellion.

HAVING stated in the FIRST PART of the NARRATIVE, that a disappointment was experienced by the forces under Lieut. Col. *Gough*, in not having the assistance and co-operation of Colonel *Gordon* in the engagement with the rebels on the twelfth of July;‡ the Editor takes this opportunity of inserting the particulars, which have been since communicated to him, and which clearly shew that the junction of the two armies was prevented by mere accident.

It appears, that upon the very same morning when Lieut. Col. *Gough* left Edenderry, in pursuit of the rebels who had retreated from Clonard, Colonel *Gordon*, who was then stationed at Trim, received information of a large body of rebels having arrived at a place called Longwood, on their route through the county of Meath, and the Colonel apprehending that much mischief might ensue, if they were suffered to remain unmolested, he marched from Trim with part of the Duke of York's Inverness Highlanders, the Trim-yeomen-cavalry and infantry, and the

‡ *See* PART *the* FIRST, *pages* 29, 30.

Rathcool

Rathcool rangers (corps that were ever prompt and zealous to act with the King's forces). Upon the approach of this body the rebels retired from Longwood to Kilmullen, setting fire to the houses of the loyalists as they passed. Every exertion was made by Colonel Gordon and his party, to come up with the rebels, but their flight was so precipitate, that the Colonel was only enabled to cut off a few straggling parties (amounting in the whole to between forty and fifty men), and after a pursuit of fifty-seven hours, darkness assisted in saving the rebels from destruction. The difficulty of getting the cannon forward, considerably retarded the progress of Colonel Gordon's march; as, from the state of the country, he could not with any prudence venture to leave them behind him.

In this manner Colonel Gordon was occupied the entire day; he had left Trim at an early hour, and was actually in chace of the rebels, when the express was dispatched from Edenderry. These facts satisfactorily account for Colonel Gordon's not receiving the express; and the flight of the enemy he pursued leading him in a direction remote from the point to which Lieut. Col. Gough moved, prevented a junction with the latter, had the former been even apprized in any part of the day of the import of the dispatch intended for him.

This

This completely explains the *fatality* ‖ alluded to in the FIRST PART of the NARRATIVE. The Editor finds, that some have thought the expression rather too strong, as implying somewhat of neglect—he is conscious that he had no such intention, his object being to detail facts without presuming to animadvert; he feels happy in this opportunity of representing the matter in its true light, and of joining his testimony to the public voice, in favour of the accomplished gentleman and gallant soldier, the *Commander of the Inverness Fencibles*.

---

*Additional Particulars relative to the Second Attack on Hacket's-town.*—See Page 190.

IN the course of the day the Rev. Mr. Brownrigg, rector of the parish (who had been in the house with Mr. Magee from the commencement of the attack) becoming anxious to hear intelligence from the barracks, as well to communicate to those who were engaged there, how effectually they were supported by Mr. Magee and his little party, walked from the house to the barracks, where he roused the desponding spirits of the almost exhausted combatants.—He had not been long there when a proposal was made by Mrs. Perry, that she should be sent to her husband accompanied by a flag of truce; which it was sup-

‖ *See* PART *the* FIRST, *page* 30.

posed

posed would put an end to the battle, but this step appeared to Mr. Brownrigg more likely to animate the rebels to greater exertions, and he accordingly resisted the proposal strenuously, which otherwise would probably have been adopted by the commanding officer.

---

*A Gentleman who headed the Loyalists requested the following should be subjoined, to which the Editor chearfully acquiesces, his primary intention being Impartiality.*

Early in the action Mrs. Hardy, mother of Captain Hardy, the wife, two grown up daughters, and a young son of Lieut. Chamney's, were taken prisoners and brought into the rebel lines, where they were witnesses of dreadful slaughter; but justice demands us to say, they were protected from any injury by General Perry and a man calling himself Col. McMahon, who conveyed them to places of safety until the action was over: the same ladies were again made prisoners at Ballyrahine, and a second time were treated with humanity by the leaders of the rebels, though in both places they were often threatened with death by the common fellows.

*FINIS.*

# A CHRONOLOGICAL TABLE

OF THE DATES OF EACH BATTLE

FOUGHT DURING

THE IRISH REBELLION, 1798,

AS DETAILED IN THIS WORK.

| Battles. | When fought. | Page. |
|---|---|---|
| Naas, | May 24, | 63 |
| Providence, | ditto | 197 |
| Kilcullen, first attack, | ditto | 65 |
| Prosperous, | ditto | 87 |
| Kilcullen, 2d attack, | ditto | 128 |
| Ballimore, | May 25, | 125 |
| Hacket's-town, | ditto | 67 |
| Monastereven, | ditto | 139 |
| Carlow, | ditto | 34 |
| Tara-hill, | May 26, | 161 |
| Leixlip, | ditto | 322 |
| Oulart, | May 27, | 98 |

Killthomas,

| Battles. | When fought. | Page. |
|---|---|---|
| Killthomas, | May 27, | 321 |
| Enniscorthy, | —— 28, | 102 |
| Rathangan, | ditto | 195 |
| Curragh of Kildare, | —— 31, | 137 |
| Newtownbarry, | June 1, | 144 |
| Tubbernerneen, | —— 4, | 120 |
| Ross, | —— 5, | 38 |
| Timahoe, | —— 8, | 9 |
| Antrim, | —— 7, | 116 |
| Saintfield, | —— 9, | 196 |
| Arklow, | ditto | 70 |
| Ballinahinch, | June 12, | 179 |
| Kilbeggan, | —— 18, | 60 |
| Kilcavan, | ditto | 187 |
| Balynascarty, | June 19, | 149 |
| Ovitstown, | ditto | 113 |
| Goff's-bridge, | June 20, | 154 |
| Vinegar-hill, | —— 21, | 75 |
| New-bridge, | —— 23, | 41 |
| Coolbawn, | ditto | 45 |
| Castlecomber, | ditto | 46 |
| Hacket's-town, | June 25, | 190 |
| Kilconnel-hill, | | |

## CHRONOLOGICAL TABLE.

| Battles. | When fought. | Page. |
|---|---|---|
| Kilconnell-hill, | June 26, | 51 |
| Fox's-hill, - | —— 29, | 11 |
| Ballyrahine-hill, | July 2, | 328 |
| Carnew, - | —— 3, | 315 |
| Clonard, - | —— 11, | 12 |
| Longwood, - | —— 12, | 324 |
| Killala, first attack, | Aug. 22, | 203 |
| Castlebar, - | —— 27, | 217 |
| Coloony, - | Sept. 5, | 264 |
| Granard, - | ditto | 244 |
| Wilson's-hospital, | Sept. 6, | 258 |
| Castlebar, 2d battle, | —— 12, | 237 |
| Ballinamuck, | —— 20, | 278 |
| Killala retaken, | —— 26, | 208 |

### ERRATA.

Page 104, line 5, for Lieut. Brien, read Prior.
Page 159, line 12, for Capt. Tatoo, read Tatlo.
Page 189, line 27, for forty Antrim, read thirty.
Page 221, line 4, for Teeling, read Roach.
Page 234, line 25, for Norcot, read Urquhart; and also through other parts of the affair of Castlebar.
Page 273, line 18, for are extracts, read is an extract.
Page 257, in note, for his son, read his nephew.

www.ingramcontent.com/pod-product-compliance
Lightning Source LLC
Chambersburg PA
CBHW030307240426
43673CB00040B/1084